THE

SANT'
EGIDIO

BOOK
OF PRAYER

I am very pleased to introduce this prayer book of the Community of Sant'Egidio, an ecclesial movement that I have known for many years. I can recommend this volume heartily. It contains so many of the answers to the most vital questions of our lives, because it moves us all along the journey to that Word who is Life itself.

Cardinal Theodore McCarrick
Archbishop Emeritus of Washington

What is the constant spiritual source in your apostolic commitment? You sing of it often in paraphrasing the words of the Apostle Peter: "We do not have riches, only the Word of the Lord." This is your strength—your trust in the feeble weapons of faith: prayer, love, and friendship. In each of your lives, let prayer always accompany your service of mercy.

Pope John Paul II
Speaking to the Community of Sant'Egidio in 1993

They pray seriously, they take the Bible seriously, and they take the poor seriously.

Cardinal Carlo Maria Martini

By living the Gospel in community, the members of Sant'Egidio demonstrate a way of growing in faith that is particularly suitable to the most vulnerable among us and to the aspirations of the young. Their journey of faith is not primarily an intellectual one but rather a path where Jesus is encountered as our friend.

Jean Vanier

In the Community of Sant'Egidio . . . prayer is the foundation of their service to the poor and their work for peace.

Olivier Clément

THE

SANT'
EGIDIO

BOOK
OF PRAYER

2009

ANDREA RICCARDI

and the Community of Sant'Egidio

ave maria press  notre dame, indiana

Founded in 1865, Ave Maria Press is a ministry of the Indiana Province of Holy Cross.

www.avemariapress.com

ISBN-10 1-59471-206-9   ISBN-13 978-1-59471-206-7

Cover image © jiunlimited.com.

Cover and text design by John R. Carson.

Printed and bound in the United States of America.

Library of Congress Cataloging-in-Publication Data

Riccardi, Andrea, 1950-
  The Sant'Egidio book of prayer / Andrea Riccardi and the Community of Sant'Egidio; foreword by Cardinal Theodore McCarrick, with an address by Pope Benedict XVI.
     p. cm.
  Includes bibliographical references.
  ISBN-13: 978-1-59471-206-7 (pbk.)
  ISBN-10: 1-59471-206-9 (pbk.)
  1. Spiritual life--Catholic Church. 2. Catholic Church--Prayers and devotions. 3. Christian life--Catholic authors. 4. Comunita di Sant'Egidio. 5. Christian communities--Catholic Church. 6. Christian communities--Italy--Sant'Egidio. I. Comunita di Sant'Egidio. II. Title.

  BX2350.3.R53 2009
  242--dc22

                        2009019651

CONTENTS

FOREWORD

I am very pleased to introduce this prayer book of the Community of Sant'Egidio, an ecclesial movement that I have known for many years. I have participated in the evening prayer of the community in the Basilica of Saint Mary in Trastevere in Rome and have been moved by the deep spirituality that one senses among the great number of people who take part in that prayer every evening.

I have come to know the founder of this community, Professor Andrea Riccardi, and have had the pleasure of speaking with him on various occasions. In particular, he and I shared the important mission bestowed on us by Pope John Paul II of bringing to the Church of Moscow the Icon of Our Lady of Kazan, which had been in the Vatican's custody for several years. This contact with Professor Riccardi gave me the opportunity to understand more fully the spirit of mission and prayer of Sant'Egidio.

Prayer is truly at the heart of the community. From it flows the love and concrete concern for the poor that characterizes the life of the community, such as the work on behalf of peace, resolving conflicts, and the dedication to interreligious dialogue. I have come to see that without this foundation of prayer, the valuable work of the community could not have given to the Church and the world the fruits that are so evident today. Sant'Egidio is now a movement that embraces more than seventy nations in the world, including the United States. In every community prayer is at the center, whether in well-known churches or in more modest settings. In every case, prayer guides the life of this community of laypeople who have generously dedicated part of their lives and their time to the poor and to the Gospel.

This book is an attempt to introduce us to this amazing community and help us pray with them as we listen to the word of God. It gives an answer to the question of how we are to pray. The confusion and the rapid pace of life today make it so much more difficult to find space for reflection and prayer, and even then it sometimes seems impossible to find the right words to speak to the Lord. Nonetheless, Jesus said to his disciples: "Be alert at all times, praying" (Lk 21:36), and the apostle Paul insists, "Rejoice always, pray without ceasing, give thanks in all circumstances; for this is the will of God in Christ Jesus for you" (1 Thess 5:16–18). This a beautiful teaching, but is it not difficult to put into practice? Jesus helps his disciples to pray, teaching them the language with which to address the Father. In the Sermon on the Mount, he says to them, "When you are praying, do not heap up empty phrases as the Gentiles do; for they think that they will be heard because of their many words" (Mt 6:7). And he teaches, "Whenever you pray, go into your room and shut the door and pray to your Father who is in secret" (Mt 6:6).

To pray it is necessary to enter your room, that is, to descend into the depths of your heart, to close the door to confusion, to the pressure of worries, and to the crowd of thoughts. We need to learn from Mary, the sister of Lazarus, who stopped her activity when Jesus entered her house so that she could sit at the feet of the Lord and listen to him, while Martha chose to press on with her domestic tasks. Prayer begins when we stop, detach ourselves from our daily cares, and take up the book of scripture. It begins when we go before the Lord and rest, listening to his words. This is the rest that each one of us needs; and the Bible is given to us in order to enlarge our hearts, strengthen our faith, and expand our love. Martha is not able to love that way because she has not listened.

To love our own sister, our own brother, it is not enough to make a fuss over them. To love it is necessary first to listen to the words that come from the mouth of the Lord. That is the one thing necessary, as Jesus said in Bethany (Lk 10:42). This book provides a path for those who wish to draw closer to God each day through prayer and meditation.

THE POWER OF PRAYER

A primary duty of every disciple is to listen to the word of God every day and to put it into practice. One Russian writer observes: "Faith without works is dead, and prayer is the first work and the principle of every true action; in it we approach God and God works in us. This is already the principle of a new spiritual life" (Solov'ev). From prayer and listening to the word of God, in fact, flows the entire life of the believer. Prayer is the source of his strength: everything is possible with prayer. To the eyes of men it may appear weak or even useless. In truth, prayer is strong: it tears down walls, seals up chasms, uproots violence, and extends the reach of mercy. Prayer is necessary for disciples and for the world because it is a powerful force for change: it destroys evil and makes love flourish. From prayer flows the power to change the world. But it must be done with faith. Not necessarily a great faith; it is sufficient, as Jesus says, merely to have faith like a mustard seed: "If you have faith the size of a mustard seed, you will say to this mountain, 'Move from here to there,' and it will move; and nothing will be impossible for you" (Mt 17:20).

All the scriptures testify that the Lord listens to prayers made with faith. Many times in the Gospels Jesus explains the importance of insistent prayer: "Ask, and it will be given you; search, and you will find; knock, and the door will be opened for you. For everyone who asks receives, and everyone who searches finds, and for everyone who knocks, the door will be opened" (Mt 7:7–8). These consoling words remind us that behind the door at which we knock is the Lord, ready to hear our petitions—even when we only manage to stammer them out.

I can recommend this volume heartily. It contains so many of the answers to the most vital questions of our lives, because it contains the words of life in so admirable a way as to move us all along the journey to that Word Who is Life itself.

Cardinal Theodore McCarrick

Introduction

⁓

The Community of
Sant'Egidio

Now the whole group of those who believed were of one heart and soul. (Acts 4:32)

On February 7, 1968, during a year of political and social upheaval both in Italy and around the world, a young man named Andrea Riccardi gathered together a small group of fellow high school students in Rome. They gathered in response to the Second Vatican Council's universal call to holiness. They gathered to pray, to take the Gospel seriously, and to meet the poor. The poor they went to meet lived in the slums on the outskirts of Rome.

While these were young students still living with their families, they recognized they had talents and that one of these talents was "culture": they could read and write, they

1

could help with math and science, and they could tutor kids in impoverished areas of the city. They moved away from the comfort of their own families to offer what they had, giving after-school classes without charge. It was the beginning of a simple, faithful "acting" on the word of God (Mt 7:24).

The young group referred to itself simply as "the community." It quickly grew in numbers, and in 1973 it was given use of an old Carmelite convent and church in the Trastevere neighborhood of Rome. Built in the early 1600s, the structure was called the Church of Sant'Egidio. It was in this church that the community's first regular, formal prayer took shape, and what had been previously called "the community" became known as "the Community of Sant'Egidio."

The Community of Sant'Egidio is gathered around the local bishops and, especially, around the Pope, the Bishop of Rome. It is a family of disciples of the Lord, a community of lay people, recognized by the Church of Rome as an association of Christians.

John Paul II said to the Community of Sant'Egidio:

> Your Community was born here, in 1968, from a group of students; it has grown in this Church of Rome which presides in charity. You developed elsewhere, inserting yourself in other local Churches, but you always maintained a marked perception of the "Roman spirit" of your origins. . . . This

characteristic of yours is not a motive of pride or privilege. It rather expresses itself in the primacy of charity that Jesus so insistently taught in the Gospel: "whoever would be first among you must be slave of all" (Mk 10:44). The Community of Sant'Egidio lived this service, according to its Statute, in evangelization, in its choice for the poor, in friendship and hospitality, in a spirit of ecumenism and dialogue . . . . Your small Community from the beginning has not given itself any other boundary than that of charity.

John Paul II concluded his speech thus:

Today's world is a land of anguish. The men and women who live in it are afraid of one another. This fear generates mutual ignorance, hostility and violence. We have to overcome this fear and its sad consequences. Your commitment to universal kinship is meant to build relationships of trust and friendship that may eradicate fear and hostility.[1]

At present the Community of Sant'Egidio is made up of over sixty thousand members located in more than seventy different countries. All the communities share some common pillars around which the life of each local community takes shape according to the needs and possibilities.

Prayer

Naming the community after the church where they prayed was not simply a designation of place. It was meant to highlight the importance prayer had in the community and its members' lives. Indeed, the first "pillar" of the Community of Sant'Egidio is prayer, in which members listen and respond to the word of God. Praying with scripture is how the community responds to Jesus' invitation to discipleship and is the source from which spring all of the community's other activities. Prayer is the beginning of a life lived for others, a life given freely and joyfully in love and service to all men and women, especially the poor.

Prayer is therefore the most authentic image of a Community of Sant'Egidio. There it becomes like the family of disciples gathered around Jesus. Coming together in common prayer is the heart of the Community of Sant'Egidio and the simple path offered to all of its members.

Prayer for the community means standing before the face of the Lord to listen to his word and to invoke his name. A great saint and martyr, Ignatius of Antioch, who died in Rome in 107 AD, and who had come to Rome as a prisoner, wrote to the Christian community of Ephesus, "For when you come frequently in the same place, the powers of Satan are destroyed, and his 'fiery darts' urging to sin fall back ineffectual. For your concord and harmonious faith prove his destruction" (XIII, 94–95). Prayer is the weak strength of the community, which it never underestimates.

Wherever the community is present in the world, its members gather as frequently as possible to pray together. Usually the prayers conclude the days, and the schedules are decided in the local communities. In many cities, the community's common prayer is open to all who wish to attend. Each member of the community is also encouraged to find a significant space for personal prayer and for reading the word of God in his or her life.

2 COMMUNICATING THE GOSPEL

The second "pillar" of the community is the communication of the Gospel. The Gospel is indeed the good news we can share with other people, the precious treasure and the light that cannot be hidden. The Gospel is not something anyone possesses; it is something we are all called to share. In the experience of the Community of Sant'Egidio, sharing and living the Gospel are synonymous with being disciples. All of the members of the Community of Sant'Egidio are called to live the joy and celebration of communicating the Good News to those in need of hope and meaning for their lives.

The communication of the Gospel is the foundation of a life of friendship open to people of different nations and cultures. Containing within itself the diversity of our world, the Community of Sant'Egidio lives in unity as a family of disciples. In a world that is building new barriers and emphasizing national and cultural differences, the communities of Sant'Egidio testify to the possibility of a common destiny for all people, not only for Christians.

SOLIDARITY WITH THE POOR

The third "pillar" of Sant'Egidio is service to the poor, lived as friendship. From the beginning, constant contact with and commitment to the poor has been a fundamental part of how Sant'Egidio responds to the call of the Gospel. The students who began the community in 1968 understood that they could not live the Gospel without being close to poor men and women. The first service, to children coming from underprivileged backgrounds, gave rise to a friendship between the rich and the poor that continues to this day.

Children are still close to the community's heart, and Schools of Peace reach out to disadvantaged children in many of the cities in which the community is present. Over the years the community has also developed a special sensitivity to old age, a nontraditional form of poverty which often condemns even the rich to loneliness and can be an added poverty for those who are materially poor. Inspired by Matthew 25, the community has widened its friendship to include other poor and marginalized people: the physically and mentally disabled, the homeless, immigrants, refugees, prisoners, and the sick, especially those who are terminally ill.

The Community of Sant'Egidio identifies with those whom the world considers the least, and it sees them as brothers and sisters, without exception. They are fully part of the community's family. Wherever there is a Community of Sant'Egidio, from Rome to San Salvador, from Cameroon to Belgium, from Ukraine to Indonesia, friendship and familiarity with poor people is always at the center of the community's life. There is no community, as well as no individual in the community, no matter how young or small, that is too weak or poor to help other poor people. Like the widow in the Gospel (Mk 12:41), every community offers what little it has to the Lord. There is "no one is so poor not to be able to serve."

The Community of Sant'Egidio's service to the poor has given rise to specific programs that unite its members and other believers and people of goodwill in efforts to combat some of the greatest evils facing the world today. Two of the community's most important projects are its campaign for a worldwide moratorium on the death penalty and DREAM (Drug Resource Enhancement against AIDS and Malnutrition), the community's program to fight AIDS in sub-Saharan Africa.

SERVICE TO PEACE

Continuous listening to the Gospel led the community to the frontier of dialogue so that all barriers could be overcome and peace could grow. Years of friendship with poor people all over the world led Sant'Egidio to understand that war is the mother of poverty. And so in many places and situations the community's love for poor people is accompanied by concrete efforts for peace. The community works to protect and rebuild peace where it is jeopardized and to facilitate dialogue where it has been lost. This work for peace and reconciliation is pursued with the weak means of prayer, solidarity, personal encounter, and dialogue.

In the midst of active conflicts, the community tries to bring humanitarian aid and assistance to the civilian populations that most suffer from war. Furthermore, some members of the community worked as mediators in the Mozambican peace process, as well as in other African countries, in Guatemala, and in the Balkans. It was through these kinds of experiences that Sant'Egidio came to believe in the weak power of prayer and in the transformative and persuasive power of non-violence. These are the attitudes that characterized Jesus' life to the end.

The Community of Sant'Egidio serves peace also through its commitment to ecumenism, which is lived out through prayer, friendship, and a desire for unity among all Christians. In addition to local initiatives, the community serves ecumenical and interfaith friendship by hosting international, interreligious meetings of prayer and dialogue in the "Spirit of Assisi," after the meeting convened in Assisi in 1986 by John Paul II.

These international meetings are inspired by the "weak strength" of peace found in all religions, a strength different from that which leads to war. At the heart of this "weak strength" there is prayer and the profound awareness that only peace is holy. The great religions must work together to build peace in the hearts and minds of believers and in public life. Dialogue among believers can also prevent and bring an end to wars and conflicts.

CULTURE OF LOVE

Years of prayer, conversation, fellowship and service to the poor, years of reflection and of contact with the world, years of welcome and love for peace have all generated an atmosphere that surrounds our communities. It is a *culture of love* that rises from the life of the communities, sanctuaries of the Gospel. The word *culture* does not refer to elitist academics, but rather to a culture that is nourished by experience, knowledge, reading, and conversation.

Culture is important because it allows one to see beyond mere personal sight. The newspaper, books, listening, and asking questions are part of this broad interest toward the world. This process of learning helps one love those who are far away and different from ourselves and to face events and realities unknown to us. Culture helps us understand that we cannot judge everything and everyone just from what we see. What is true spiritually, "Do not judge, so that you may not be judged" (Mt 7:1), reveals also its wisdom and sensitivity in building a culture that is tolerant and open to the other.

The culture of love is a language built over the years that helps the community to understand the world. It is the youth of the eyes and of the heart as the years pass. When pride and natural strength of youth diminish or vanish, culture becomes dialogue with the other, with their history, with their world.

The culture of the community is grounded in prayer. As such, the following is, first and foremost, a prayer book. It offers an introduction to the life of a Christian community and its work, but before all other "works," it is the community's prayer that is the source and service to others. Prayer is what makes fruitful all of rest of the community's life—it is in prayer that we "receive his love and learn his ways."

PART ONE

THE GOSPEL
AND THE
COMMUNITY

MEETING JESUS

⁓

Near the shore of the lake of Gennesaret, which the Gospels sometimes call the Sea of Galilee, there is a man speaking to a group of people. At a certain moment, the man notices two boats that have pulled up onto the shore and the fishermen who are getting off the boats. The man approaches the boats, gets into one of them, and asks Simon (one of the fishermen and the boat's owner), to go out into the boat with him a little way so that he can better speak to the people. The man is called Jesus of Nazareth, and he is a well-known teacher in Galilee, known both for his preaching and for the things he does. Simon agrees, and placing the boat a little way from the shore, Jesus starts to speak to his listeners from it. When he finishes speaking, Jesus asks Simon: "put out into the deep water and let down your nets for a catch" (Lk 5:4).

It is probable that Simon did not know Jesus well. He may have heard of Jesus because of the miracles Jesus performed in various places around Galilee, but that was their first real meeting, a moment of discovery and transformation. Jesus was not Simon's relative, nor was he a friend, nor did he have any real authority over Simon. He did not have anything to give Simon in return for the use of his boat. Nevertheless, Jesus asked something of Simon. Jesus asked Simon to go out into the deep with him—he wanted Simon to collaborate with him.

Maybe it seemed just a casual request, but with that encounter on the shore of the lake of Gennesaret, Jesus entered into Simon's life. The encounter was one of many Simon had during the course of his life, but this event proved decisive for him. From that moment, Simon's life began to change. By the end of that day, Simon began to call Jesus "master"(Lk 5:5), a title normally given by Jews to those who explained the word of God. In using this term, Simon instinctively acknowledged that Jesus had a lot to teach him.

Simon had, in fact, found a master. Before meeting Jesus, he likely thought he had nothing more to learn, having already learned how to be a good fisherman. On the contrary, throughout his life, Simon would have much to learn from Jesus, and he would have much to listen to. And if Jesus was the Master, then Simon was a disciple. Simon, an expert at his job and probably well-known in his small hometown of Capernaum as such, becomes a disciple, like he did when he was at school or when he was first learning his job. When he meets Jesus, an adult man becomes a disciple again. In fact, all those who are Christians are disciples for all their lives—there are always new things to learn.[2]

Simon had also met a friend, someone he would become profoundly attached to—so much so that he remained attached to him even after Jesus' death. Simon would never forget Jesus' name. The name of Jesus became something decisive for him. Simon would rejoice with Jesus; he would cry at his denial of Jesus. That friendly presence would never abandon his life. In Jesus he had found a master, a consoler, and a man who was able to understand everything about him.

In Jesus, Simon had met a great, new presence. Initially, he was not able to define this presence with words. But one day, long after that first meeting on the lake of Gennesaret, when their friendship had grown, Jesus asked him: "Who do people say that the Son of Man is? . . . who do you say that I am?" (Mt 16:13,15). Simon's answer came from his heart. He had listened to Jesus, and he had loved him. Because of this, he was finally able to express with words the meaning of that great presence he perceived in the Master of Nazareth: "You are the Messiah, the Son of the living God" (Mt 16:16). Simon had understood that Jesus of Nazareth was the Son of God. He had found the words of faith.

The story of Jesus and Simon, though beautiful and essential to our faith, is but one beautiful page from the Gospels.[3] Jesus has allowed others to find him along the roads of the world. Encounters with Jesus continue, even in our own time. It is not Simon who meets Jesus today, but men and women from everywhere, young and old alike. The encounter does not take place on the lake of Gennesaret, but in countries all over the world—in distant lands, among people of very different languages and cultures; but the encounter does continue to take place. The word of Jesus continues to be addressed to men and women of all times and places. Of course, people do not always recognize him immediately. At times they continue on their way, but at others, they experience the same amazement, the same feelings that Simon experienced.

These meetings with Jesus can take place in a variety of ways. Sometimes, the encounter is turbulent, as it was for Paul, who was persecuting the disciples: a light flashed about him, he fell to the ground, and he heard a voice saying "Saul, Saul, why do you persecute me?" (Acts 9:4). At other times, Jesus invites people by saying, "Follow me," as he said to Philip (Jn 1:43), and to Matthew while he was seated at the tax booth (Mt 9:9). The men and women who meet Jesus are very different from one another: they are different in age; their meetings with Jesus happen in very different ways. But Jesus continues to let men and women find him on the roads of the world. He lets himself be found even after his death, resurrection, and ascension to heaven. Paul, as we said, meets him on the road to Damascus, long after Jesus' ascension. The Acts of the Apostles is the story of the many meetings of men and women with the word of Jesus that is communicated by his disciples. Jesus said to his disciples, "Whoever listens to you listens to me" (Lk 10:16). *Where one meets the disciples of Jesus, there one meets the word of the Master.*

Meeting Jesus still takes place today on the roads of the world. It happens for many men and women who, like Simon, are disillusioned because of a night, or a day, or of an entire life without fruit. To them, like Simon, the Master asks to go out into the deep, away from the ordinary way they live, and confront their own frustrations and perplexities. Jesus says to them, "Do not be afraid," and like Simon, they begin to sense in Jesus a master, a friend.

DIALOGUE WITH JESUS

Sometimes, one's vivid perception of Jesus as Master weakens. Other times we forget this perception of faith entirely. But dialogue with Jesus, and closeness to his disciples, can enliven our faith. Jesus asked Simon to go out into the deep to cast nets in a lake that Simon knew well—he had been working there a long time. That lake was his environment and his world. There he earned bread for himself and for his family. Jesus knew the lake less well, but he nevertheless asked Simon to start fishing again after a night in which they had not been able to catch anything. Faced with this request, Simon showed resistance. Was this fear? Weariness? Negative experiences? His experience told him that another effort would be useless.

Simon did not hide his resistance from Jesus: "Master, we have worked all night long but have caught nothing" (Lk 5:5). Simon is not immediately won over by Jesus' idea. But he doesn't say no to him either. Simon does what Jesus asks because he is beginning to perceive that Jesus may know better. This is why he confesses his earlier difficulties but then adds: "Yet if you say so, I will let down the nets." The word of Jesus was in fact beginning to touch him. Simon was not simply responding to an interesting man or an unusual teacher. This was something more. Jesus spoke in a very special way. His words were the words of someone who spoke with authority.

It is not only the experience of Simon, who at the word of Jesus casts his nets, obtaining a prodigious catch. The crowds who hear the important words of Jesus, words that are generally called "the Sermon on the Mount," have the same experience. At the end of Jesus' sermon, we read in the Gospel of Matthew, "the crowds were astounded at his teaching, for he taught them as one having authority, and not as their scribes" (Mt 7:28–29). Jesus' words were truly special; they were different from the ones they were used to hearing. His words were neither common nor ordinary, as were those of the scribes (that is, the intellectuals) of their time.

In the episode of the lake of Gennesaret, Simon witnesses an event he considered unlikely: a great catch, after a whole night at sea without success. The fish were so many that they feared the nets would break. We read in the Gospel of Luke: "For he and all who were with him were amazed" (Lk 5:9). Astonishment often accompanies those who meet Jesus and his word. It is an encounter the disciples had never had before. Simon perceives that he has met someone greater than himself. He is shaken. He thus feels the need to talk to Jesus about his life in an intimate way: "Go away from me Lord, for I am a sinful man!" (Lk 5:8). When he meets Jesus and listens to his words, Simon is moved to confess that he is a sinner. Encountering such a great presence and hearing such effective words, Simon feels that he is small, and most of all a sinner.

Maybe Simon is thinking about his past life, about his meager heart, about his old feelings. He is a sinner. Jesus probably just does not know him well enough. Jesus is likely wrong to want him around. Simon feels he is not worthy to be close to people of Jesus' importance, to follow him and to live the life Jesus lives. But the sinner is not the "wrong" man—someone who cannot approach Jesus. *There is nobody who is unsuitable to be with Jesus, and no one is unworthy to receive his word.* Neither education, nor character, nor one's own past, nor culture make a man or a woman suitable to be near the Lord.

Still, in his dialogue with Jesus, Simon realizes he is a sinner. Because of this, he says to Jesus, with sincerity, "Go away from me." But Jesus came for sinners—people like Simon, like all the other disciples, like all of us. He in fact says: "I have come to call not the righteous but sinners" (Mt 9:13). A disciple is a sinner who has met Jesus and has been forgiven by him. Moreover, a disciple, throughout his or her own life, always needs the forgiveness of the Lord.[4]

The more disciples listen to the Master, the more they understand themselves, their sin, and the Lord's love.

Jesus does not recoil from sin or from the problems of the people he meets. The Gospels are stories of the direct encounters of Jesus with sin and sinners. They tell of Jesus' meetings with people who were full of problems of all kinds, with those who were sick, with the insane who appeared possessed, with circumstances that were considered irresolvable, with people like the lepers who were rejected by virtually everyone. No problem keeps Jesus away, neither sin nor human insufficiency. No power of evil keeps him away. Jesus approaches everyone. He speaks to everyone.

The disciple continually discovers something new when listening to the word of Jesus. The newness and the welcome and the authority of Jesus are felt not just at the beginning, like with Simon on the boat, but all throughout the disciple's life. We see this in the Gospel of John, which ends with an intimate talk between the risen Jesus and Simon (Jn 21:15–23). We see it in the crowd, who continually wanted to listen to his word (Lk 5:1). For this reason, the Church has always venerated the word of the Lord and has offered it to Christians as good nourishment for their lives.[5]

Like every disciple, Simon, after having listened to the word of the Lord, discovers the need to change his life and be forgiven. At the same time, he worries that this is not possible or that it will be very difficult. Maybe he thinks that his sin is too great to be forgiven.[6] Maybe he thinks his character is too difficult to become a disciple of a Master who is so good. Maybe he is convinced that there is little to be done with him, an adult man with consolidated habits. But Jesus continues to speak to him and continues to forgive him. He consoles him by saying, "Do not be afraid; from now on you will be catching people" (Lk 5:10).

THE GOSPEL

Every disciple reads the Gospel "apart," that is, in silence, and tries to live it among people amid everyday life. The disciples make the word of Jesus the heart of their existence. On this path, they liberate themselves from the sad and violent habits they have often been educated to; they free themselves from the bad feelings that sometimes permeate them, and they are liberated from self-love. In other words, disciples find a new way of looking at life and at others. Throughout their lives, disciples are called to renew themselves. This should apply wherever the disciples live, both within every community and in the larger world: on the streets, in the family, at work, when important decisions are made, when speaking. The apostle Paul exhorts Christians to live not according to what appear to be the hard rules of daily life, not to surrender to these rules, especially when they seem obvious or taken for granted: "See that none of you repays evil for evil" (1 Thess 5:15).

The Gospel helps us to look at others, and at life, in a different way. Living the Gospel, there are no enemies to fight. There is no one to hate. There is no one to be despised because they are different or poor. No one is to be avoided. No one is to be condemned.

Jesus looked at men and women with love, overcoming the prejudices of his time. Prejudices, inherited from our environment, are like walls separating us from others. Sometimes they appear insurmountable. Jesus was accused of being a friend of sinners, of talking with prostitutes, of associating himself with people of dubious reputation. And it was true: Jesus was a friend to all men and women. For him there were no strangers or foreigners. He did not even shun the people of his town who rejected him, or even those who occupied important places and often attacked him. We see this in the long talks with the scribes and the pharisees. Jesus looks at everyone with love. Thus, the disciples are called to live with openness and friendship, most of all with sensitivity, among the people. They, in fact, can be recognized by this attitude of openness and of the rejection of prejudices.

In the Gospel of Matthew, before the call of the twelve apostles and their instruction in mission, we read that Jesus went around to many towns and villages, "teaching in their synagogues, and proclaiming the good news of the kingdom, and curing every disease and every sickness"

(Mt 9:35). We find in this chapter a true image of Jesus. We see how he looked at the people he met on his travels: "When he saw the crowds, he had compassion for them, because they were harassed and helpless, like sheep without a shepherd" (Mt 9:36).

Jesus looked at people with compassion. He understood that, despite appearances, many of them were tired, exhausted. In their daily lives, they had no guide, no help, and no reference: they were very much like sheep without a shepherd. The compassion and the emotion with which Jesus looked at the crowds were neither shallow nor sentimental—it was an attitude of profound participation in their situation and in their suffering.

From the compassion of Jesus came his way of living among the crowds. He spent his life with and for them, with and for those who were harassed and helpless, like sheep without a shepherd. Jesus gave them what he had. *Jesus preached the Gospel and cured every sickness,* as the Gospel says. Preaching the Gospel and healing those who are sick and weak is the very heart of his mission, the deepest expression of his compassion for the crowds.

The disciples in turn became involved in the Lord's love for the people. What Jesus said to his disciples in front of the hungry multitude is repeated today: "You give them something to eat" (Mk 6:37). These words are addressed to us. How is this possible? How is it possible to help those who are weak, those who are infirm? How do we take care of them? How is it possible to communicate the Gospel to people who seem to be consumed by other problems and not very interested in listening?

In many parts of the Gospel, Jesus addresses the disciples so that they will learn to do what he has done. He himself is looking for people willing to collaborate with him because "the harvest is plentiful, but the laborers are few" (Mt 9:37), as he says after having seen the crowds. Today, as then, in every corner of the world, Jesus is searching for men and women who can share in his compassion and who can work with him. But in order to work with him, we have to share his life. Jesus himself, as we read in the Gospel of Matthew, gives to his apostles the power to cast out demons and to heal every kind of disease and infirmity. At the end of this same Gospel, the risen Jesus solemnly says to his people, "Go therefore and make disciples of all nations" (Mt 28:19). *The way of the disciple is that of sharing Jesus' attitude toward the crowds, to communicate the Gospel, and to care for those who are infirm.*

What can the disciples say to the crowds? It is a question that we often ask ourselves. We ask it of ourselves when we confront difficult situations, people who appear to be more educated than we are, people who seem indifferent or concerned about things other than the Gospel. It is a question that the first disciples of Jesus were asking themselves as well. Do people really need the Gospel? In the First Letter of Peter we hear what is likely a response to such questions—questions that Christians of that time were asking themselves amidst many anxieties: "Do not fear what they fear, and do not be intimidated, but in your hearts sanctify Christ as Lord. Always be ready to make your defense to anyone who demands from you an accounting for the hope that is in you" (1 Pt 3:14–15).

The brothers and sisters are exhorted to always be prepared to account for that hope they have in their heart. *The faith of Christians is not something hidden or inexplicable.* A community that does not communicate its faith does not take part in the compassion of the Lord for the crowds. A silent and fearful disciple does not look at the people with the same eyes as the Lord but hides behind the walls of prejudice, of well-being, or of his habits. The Lord helps us to see in others, rich or poor, beyond their appearances, people who are in need. Many have not found the shepherd of their life. Moreover, the lives of many have been the prey of thieves and mercenaries and have thus been thrown away, wasted, or stolen. There is suffering and poverty in them, even if it is hidden behind riches and security.

Jesus says: "I am the good shepherd. The good shepherd lays down his life for the sheep" (Jn 10:11). And he adds, "I am the good shepherd; I know my own and my own know me" (Jn 10:14). In the similitude of the good shepherd, Jesus compares himself to the guardian of the sheep: "He calls his own sheep by name and leads them out. When he has brought out all his own, he goes ahead of them, and the sheep follow him because they know his voice" (Jn 10:3–4). To communicate the Gospel means to enable others to recognize the voice of the Lord and to find in him the shepherd of their life. It means to help others to live the encounter with Jesus, the one that for Simon took place on the lake of Gennesaret when he heard the voice of the Lord. It means to help others live the encounter that has taken place in our lives as well.

There are many ways to communicate the Gospel to the people of today. The scriptures themselves offer many different ways by which the community communicates the Gospel. Cultures and people's situations may change with the centuries. However, there is something that does not change: we must never stop announcing the Gospel and must never stop being moved by the people who have no shepherd. To be sure, not everyone will recognize the voice of the Lord in the witness we give, in the account we give of our hope, in the life we live. Others will be interested and enthusiastic, but they will have to be helped to persevere in listening—we do not become disciples of the Lord in a day. Yet others will be attracted but will be afraid to change something in their lives, like the rich young man who went to Jesus to ask what he should do but went away sad because he was afraid. For some, the time has not yet come to open their hearts. Others will find what they are looking for and follow the shepherd.

The parable of the sower speaks about the experience of the communication of the word of Jesus (Mt 13:3–23). The sower is the one who communicates the word of God. The seed does not always bear fruit: sometimes the devil steals the word of God; sometimes it is forgotten because of trials and difficulties; at other times, it is suffocated under the cares of life. But Jesus says that there is also a word that is sown upon good ground: "as for what was sown on good soil, this is the one who hears the word and understands it, who indeed bears fruit and yields, in one case a hundredfold, in another sixty, and in another thirty" (Mt 13:23). Each one of us who has listened to the word of the Lord and tried to put it into practice has lived the same experience of that seed that fell on the good ground. In the scripture there are many people who open their hearts to the Gospel as the good ground welcomes the seed.

Paul, in his many travels to preach the Gospel, goes to Philippi and remains several days in that city. He speaks of the Gospel to some women, and one, called Lydia, a merchant, listened to his word: "The Lord," we read in the Acts of the Apostles, "opened her heart to listen eagerly to what was said by Paul" (Acts 16:14). The Acts testify that Paul and his friends found difficulties and refusals in Philippi as well. However, a beautiful community was born in that city, a community that the apostle Paul returned to visit afterward. We can understand something about the life of this community from the Letter to the Philippians that Paul wrote while he was in prison. But everything started on that day in which the apostle spoke and in which the Lord opened the heart of Lydia, a trader, to his words.

Sometimes, when one meets with people's indifference, one may be tempted to say that they are not suitable for the Gospel; they are not made to believe. We can be quick to make evaluations and to judge. But one forgets that each one of us is proof that it is possible for the seed to fall on good ground. Among the many people we encounter, there is always a Lydia. And even then, it is the Lord who opens the heart. For this the disciple must be patient. One must not look for immediate success or lose heart if it does not quickly come.

The Letter of James, addressed to a community that most likely lived among many difficulties, shows how Christian life is one of patience: "Be patient, therefore, beloved, until the coming of the Lord. The farmer waits for the precious crop from the earth, being patient with it until it receives the early and the late rains" (Jas 5:7).[7]

Patience is the daily bread of the disciple. For the disciples there is no victory that can free them from tomorrow's labor; there is no success that makes them dismiss their own responsibility for a while. Besides, to communicate the Gospel is not like selling a product for which you can speak about success or failure. To communicate the Gospel is not advertising. We speak because we believe, and sometimes we must believe more in order to be able to communicate better to others. We communicate what we have lived in our hearts and in our lives so that everyone may hear the voice of the Lord. The Lord himself will eventually open the heart.

It is not always easy to communicate the Gospel. Sometimes one can feel discouraged. At other times one may face difficult situations. Even in the most difficult situations one must not worry too much: "do not worry about how you are to speak or what you are to say," says Jesus to those disciples who are sent to preach the Gospel, "for what you are to say will be given to you at that time; for it is not you who speak, but the Spirit of your Father speaking through you" (Mt 10:19–20).

To communicate the Gospel is to enable others to listen to the voice of the Lord and find the shepherd for their lives. Only in this way will they understand what it means to be disciples. This is how the Spirit speaks to their willing hearts. To communicate the Gospel does not mean to be boastful or aggressive. The disciples of the Lord can be recognized by their meekness.[8] They are not boastful people who despise everyone. Paul tells the Philippians, "Let your gentleness be known to everyone" (Phil 4:5); while he says to the people of Colossae, "Conduct yourselves wisely toward outsiders, making the most of the time. Let your speech always be gracious, seasoned with salt, so that you may know how you ought to answer everyone" (Col 4:5–6). In the First Letter of Peter, after instructing the disciples to always be ready to account for their hope, we read: "Yet do it with gentleness and reverence" (1 Pt 3:15).

The Spirit of the Lord helps the disciples to communicate the Gospel. After Pentecost, those who were in Jerusalem heard the words of Simon Peter in their native tongue. It was not Peter who was speaking all languages, but the Spirit who was coming to his aid. The Spirit knows the language of the heart and speaks to the hearts of those who listen. The Spirit also speaks by showing the needs of the others and those of the poor: faced with all this, sometimes, one understands the call to live a more generous life. Often the poor are a living reminder for us not to worry only about ourselves.

Every community is called to communicate the Gospel so that everyone is moved in the same way Jesus was moved when he faced the people. Indeed, still today Jesus sees the crowds of this world, and he understands how poor they are, even when they think they are well or rich. There is a misery in some of those who are well and who have everything. Today, as in his own day, the word of Jesus explains the malaise of so many of these people. It comes from the absence of a true shepherd for their lives. Because of this absence, many live in a disoriented way, even though they do not believe they do. Jesus continues to say to us, with a great love for the people: "The harvest is plentiful, but the laborers are few" (Lk 10:2).

CONVERSION

Fifty days after the resurrection of Jesus, on the day of Pentecost, Simon, who had been named Peter by Jesus, spoke to the people of Jerusalem. For many who were listening, it was their first encounter with Jesus' word. We read in the second chapter of the Acts of the Apostles, "Now when they heard this, they were cut to the heart and said to Peter and the other apostles, `Brothers, what should we do?'" (Acts 2:37). The preaching of the word of Jesus touches the heart. We see this in the story of the two disciples who, soon after the death of Jesus, were walking, disillusioned, from Jerusalem to Emmaus. After their conversation with a mysterious companion, they said to one another, "Were not our hearts burning within us while he was talking to us on the road?" (Lk 24:32). Their traveling companion was Jesus. His word had caused their hearts to burn and had spoken to their sadness.

The encounter with the word of Jesus touches the heart and leads to a question. The people of Jerusalem asked Simon Peter: "What should we do?" Those who feel their heart touched cannot continue to do things as they did them before. Those who feel their heart touched search for a new life, or at the very least they ask themselves what they should do now. This is why Jesus and his disciples talk about repentance and conversion. To repent is to recognize that the life we were leading up to that moment was not a good one: it is to recognize our sin, our lack of love, and our lack of faith. Simon repents in front of Jesus when he discovers himself to be a sinner. Simon, who has experienced repentance since the lake of Gennesaret, says to the people of Jerusalem: "Repent, and be baptized every one of you in the name of Jesus Christ so that your sins may be forgiven" (Acts 2:38).

What is there to do? Jesus' answer is repentance and conversion. Since the very beginning of his preaching, when he was still alone and he had not yet even met his first disciples, he began to say: "Repent, for the kingdom of heaven has come near" (Mt 4:17). Conversion is to change one's life and to begin to follow the Lord, to follow Jesus and not oneself or one's habits. Conversion is to begin to listen to his word and not only to one's own thoughts. Conversion is to become a disciple of Jesus, and one encounter alone is not enough; encounters with Jesus continue for the whole of one's life. Conversion is not merely something that occurs at the beginning of discipleship. If we are to continue to be disciples, we have to continue to convert to the Lord, which means to continue to change our way of thinking and our way of living.[9]

Those who hear the word of Jesus ask: "What should we do?" They ask because they understand that they cannot continue to live as they always have. They ask because they would like to live better and to be better. Through repentance, they come to see that they have been dominated by self-love. They haven't loved others much, were not really aware of them, and in many cases even trampled upon them. They lived for themselves. Thus, those who undergo repentance want to be freed from self-love and from their old feelings.[10]

Maximus the Confessor, a father of the Church and a Christian who had a great experience of conversion, wrote, "Those who reject the mother of all passions, that is, self-love, easily refuse, with the help of God, all other passions: rage, sadness, rancor" (*Centuries on Love* 2:8). A rich young man went to Jesus asking what he should do. Jesus reminded him of the commandments in the Hebrew scriptures, but the young man answered that he had observed them all from youth. Jesus then asked him to abandon his riches, but the young man could not do it. In fact, he went away sad because he loved himself and his riches too much (Mt 19:16–22).

Conversion calls us to abandon self-love and to live out a greater love. To follow Jesus is to begin to live a love that is greater than that for oneself, greater than "*filautia.*"

In the first chapter of the Gospel of John we read about two men (one of them was Andrew, the brother of Simon Peter) who heard Jesus speak and approached him. The passage states, "When Jesus turned and saw them following, he said to them, 'What are you looking for?' They said to him, 'Rabbi' (which translated means Teacher), 'where are you staying?' He said to them, 'Come and see.' They came and saw where he was staying, and they remained with him that day" (Jn 1:38–39). Conversion is following Jesus. It is to start to follow him, and it is to continue to follow him, because on his way we discover a greater love. But to follow him, we have to ask him where he lives, where his house is. We then have to remain with him. Only in this way can we be close to him.

The two disciples went to Jesus' house on the very same day in which they had begun to follow him. They stayed with him. In that house a small community was formed: Jesus and two disciples. Community is staying with the Lord and his disciples. Jesus said: "For where two or three are gathered in my name, I am there among them" (Mt 18:20). Conversion to the Lord unites us to brothers and sisters, to the disciples of Jesus who form his family.

The two crestfallen disciples, the ones who were walking between Jerusalem and Emmaus after the crucifixion, changed their path after they recognized Jesus. They went back to reunite with the community of Jerusalem: "That same hour they got up and returned to Jerusalem; and they found the eleven and their companions gathered together" (Lk 24:33).

After Peter's speech at Pentecost, we read in Acts, "and that day about three thousand persons were added" (Acts 2:41). Conversion carries us closer to the Lord. It carries us into his house and among his people.

Community

After Jesus began to preach, a family of disciples gathered around him. It was his community. This community was made up of those who met him and were converted to his word. In the Gospel of Luke, we find a portrait of the community gathered around Jesus:

> He went on through cities and villages, proclaiming and bringing the good news of the kingdom of God. The twelve were with him, as well as some women who had been cured of evil spirits and infirmities: Mary, called Magdalene, from whom seven demons had gone out, and Joanna, the wife of Herod's steward Chuza, and Susanna, and many others, who provided for them out of their resources. (Lk 8:1–3)

In this community there were men and women. There were people to whom Jesus entrusted great responsibilities, such as Simon Peter; there were others whose names are not remembered. This community becomes the family of Jesus. To be part of it there is no need to be a relative of Jesus, no need to be his countryman, no need to have special talents. It is enough to listen with the heart, to follow him, and to do his word. It is enough to ask him, "Where do you live?"

One time there were a lot of people crowding in around Jesus. His mother and his brothers were there too, but they were not able to get close to him because the crowd was pressing him from all sides. Someone then told him about his relatives' presence, saying, "Your mother and your brothers are standing outside, wanting to see you" (Lk 8:20). Jesus answered, "My mother and my brothers are those who hear the word of God and do it" (Lk 8:21). *The family of Jesus is those who hear his word and do it.*[11] By means of conversion and through listening to the word of Jesus, we become part of his family. There is no birthright to discipleship; it is enough to listen and to follow the Lord.[12]

We read elsewhere that Jesus, looking around at those who were close to him, said, "Here are my mother and my brothers! Whoever does the will of God is my brother and sister and mother" (Mk 3:34–35). Among the disciples Jesus was looking at were Simon, Andrew, the women, and others. But Jesus does not look only at them, but also at many other families that would be gathered by his word in every corner of the world. Jesus says to everyone who will listen, "Here are my mother and my brothers! Whoever does the will of God is my brother and sister and mother." By following Jesus today, as his first disciples did, we become companions of his disciples, members of his family.

On the day of Pentecost, Peter said to those who had been touched by his words, "Repent, and be baptized every one of you in the name of Jesus Christ so that your sins may be forgiven; and you will receive the gift of the Holy Spirit" (Acts 2:38). Today, some who hear the word of Jesus have already received baptism, often when they were children—but they did not become disciples of Jesus, and they have not followed his way. Sometimes they have not met anyone who would show them the way. Their baptism deeply marked them and set them apart to live with the Lord, but they now need to revive baptism's gifts. Some others have not received baptism, even if, maybe vaguely, they have heard about the Gospel. These people are called to walk the way that would carry them to baptism.[13]

Conversion impels us to join the community of the disciples of the Lord. "Lord, where do you live?" He lives in the house of the Lord, with his family. In the life of the community the disciples will receive many gifts: "You will receive the gift of the Holy Spirit," says Peter (Acts 2:38). The Spirit opens the heart to love. The hearts of the disciples become broader. with a more profound comprehension of the word of God. The Spirit liberates the heart from self-love and opens it to love for the brothers and sisters. This is why the Acts of the Apostles describes the community of Jerusalem as follows: "Now the whole group of those who believed were of one heart and soul" (Acts 4:32).

In the Acts of the Apostles, we find another portrait of the community: "They went to the room upstairs where they were staying, Peter, and John, and James, and Andrew, Philip and Thomas, Bartholomew and Matthew, James son of Alphaeus and Simon the Zealot and Judas son of James. All these were constantly devoting themselves to prayer, together with certain women, including Mary the mother of Jesus, as well as his brothers" (Acts 1:13–14). This is the first community—the one that formed after the Lord ascended to heaven. It is joined by those who encountered the word of the Lord. *To convert means, for a man and a woman, to become part of this family, with one accord devoted to prayer, gathered around the apostles, their witness and their preaching.*

Over time, the preaching of the word of Jesus has generated many communities in the world. In various times and places, the Spirit has descended upon brothers and sisters who have opened their hearts. These are the communities of the disciples. In Antioch, as we read in the Acts of the Apostles, the people began to give these disciples the name of "Christians" for the first time. They are the first Christian communities.

These communities are families of discipleship united in love. Jesus looks at these disciples of his who are seated around him to hear his word and says: "My mother and my brothers are those who hear the word of God and do it." The family is a family of disciples. A Christian always remains a disciple of Jesus. He is a disciple at the beginning, when he meets the Master. As the years pass, he remains a disciple. We never cease being disciples in the Christian life. This is why Jesus admonishes those Christians who believe they have already heard enough and now only have to teach others: "But you are not to be called rabbi, for you have one teacher, and you are all students" (Mt 23:8).

THE JOY OF BEING
CHRISTIANS TODAY

⁓

In the Gospel of Luke, we read a story in which Jesus sends out a large number of disciples on mission. The text states that upon completing their mission, "The seventy-two returned with joy, saying, 'Lord, in your name even the demons submit to us!'" (Lk 10:17). Those seventy-two disciples had been sent by Jesus to live the life of the Gospel among the people. They did so, and they returned full of joy. The disciples experienced something they considered impossible before they met Jesus—just as Peter had considered it impossible to catch fish that day on the lake of Gennesaret. They experienced for themselves that in Jesus' name, demons were subjected and people were healed.

Jesus himself takes part in the joy of his disciples. He tells them, "I watched Satan fall from heaven like a flash of lightning" (Lk 10:18), and goes on to rejoice in the Holy Spirit, exclaiming, "I thank you, Father, Lord of heaven and earth, because you have hidden these things from the wise and the intelligent and have revealed them to infants" (Lk 10:21).

The joy of these seventy-two disciples lives on. It is not simply a story from the past. *We today can live and experience the joy of being Christians.* Of course there were serious difficulties that the early Christian generations faced. Recent generations of Christians have faced them as well. The Community of Sant'Egidio treasures the memory of those who lost their lives for the sake for the Gospel. Encouraged by their testimony, the community lives, with all the difficulties and all the weakness of its members, the joy of being Christians.[14]

When the community gathers in prayer, the disciples present themselves to the Lord. We present ourselves to the Lord with what we have done: how we have helped those who were ill, have spoken of the Gospel, have lived in friendship with many people, have been brothers and sisters among ourselves, how we have been weak and sinful.

The Lord, too, rejoices today, as he did when the seventy-two disciples returned. He rejoices because there are little ones who understand his "things." Others, though intelligent and wise, close their hearts. The community tries to understand the "things" of the Lord, listening to his word and living his love among the people.

The fact that the community gathers together in prayer and friendship shows that it has understood the one "thing" that Jesus considers crucial. The "thing" is this: *that the disciples are to be brothers and sisters and that they should consider themselves a community.* In the very last moments of Jesus' life with his community, just before he is betrayed by Judas, Jesus says to his disciples: "I give you a new commandment, that you love one another. Just as I have loved you, you also should love one another" (Jn 13:34). Christian fellowship is a decisive characteristic of the community. Jesus' insistence on fellowship is so strong that he makes it the very basis of the community: "By this everyone will know that you are my disciples, if you have love for one another" (Jn 13:35). Real fellowship among peoples of different languages and different ethnic groups, who have started to listen to the word of Jesus and who love one another: this is proof that they truly are disciples of Jesus.

The community that gathers around the Lord reveals that the brothers and sisters understood another decisive "thing": *they understood that Jesus is their Master and nothing must be placed before him.* They consider him their friend, and they do not place anything before his advice. The Lord Jesus, we believe, rejoices when he sees that his disciples understand these "things" revealed by the Father.

The Lord Jesus exults when he sees that his disciples are walking joyfully on their path.

The fact that the brothers and sisters of the community love those who suffer shows that they have understood yet another "thing" of the Lord. The "thing" is this: *that we must not live for ourselves, dominated by self-love, but that we must love other men and women, especially those who suffer most.*

The Community of Sant'Egidio wants to be a community that takes these "things" to heart, *to love one another as brothers and sisters, to love everyone and especially those who are the weakest, to communicate the Gospel, to put nothing before the Lord, to gather around him in prayer.* To live these "things" there is no need to be intelligent or wise; it is enough to hear and do Jesus' word.

By living in this way, we discover the joy of being Christians, as Andrea Riccardi said in his address to Benedict XVI on the occasion of the pope's visit to the Church of St. Bartholomew, where the Community treasures the relics of the new martyrs: "We have discovered the joyful and responsible gift of a charisma. It is what we are glad to tell your Holiness: we are happy to be Christians and to be children of the Church! We say it with a cry of joy louder than the cries of sorrow, that we nevertheless hear in the world. Yes, we are happy to be Christians!"

PRAYER

Sometimes, disciples forget that they belong to a family and that they have a loving father. They become instead like orphans. Someone who lives his or her discipleship like an orphan does not remember the word of the Lord, the love of the brothers and sisters, or the responsibility to be merciful. Often, those who live in this way are seized by anguish for themselves and for their own lives. But the Father does not forget his children: "And do not keep striving for what you are to eat and what you are to drink, and do not keep worrying. For it is the nations of the world that strive after all these things, and your Father knows that you need them" (Lk 12:29–30). And before he left his disciples, in the farewell speech of the Gospel of John, Jesus firmly restates: "I will not leave you orphaned; I am coming to you" (Jn 14:18).

Prayer is the gathering of the disciples with the Father.
When disciples pray, they are gathered both among themselves and with their Master. They gather as the family of God. Jesus gathered with them in prayer when he invited the disciples to come and spend some time away with him in a quiet place. The life of the disciples is not only preaching to the crowds and healing the sick; there are also moments in which the family gathers together, alone with Jesus, to listen to him and to pray. They are the moments "apart," away from the crowds. One of these moments is the supper Jesus eats with his disciples before being arrested. During that supper Jesus commands his disciples to meet and celebrate his presence and the memory of him in the bread and in the chalice. It is the Eucharist that the Church faithfully continues to celebrate, confessing the presence of the Lord. The Eucharist is the heart of the life of the Church. Every time we celebrate the Eucharist, we remember the death and resurrection of the Lord, who is truly present in the cup of blessing and in the bread of the supper.[15]

In these moments apart, Jesus' disciples ask him: "Lord, teach us to pray" (Lk 11:1). Jesus was a man of prayer, and he often withdrew to pray. Various accounts of Jesus' life of prayer can be found in the Gospels. Once, "during those days [Jesus] went out to the mountain to pray; and he spent the night in prayer to God" (Lk 6:12). In the Gospel of Mark, we read that one morning in Capernaum, "In the morning, while it was still very dark, [Jesus] got up and went out to a deserted place, and there he prayed" (Mk 1:35). Seeing him pray, the disciples ask Jesus to teach them to pray. Often Christians do not know how to pray because prayer is a language that has to be learned.

Jesus teaches prayer to his disciples. The Gospels relate the text of the prayer the Lord taught his disciples, the Our Father, which is the first prayer of the community. Sometimes Christians say that it is more important to do the right thing than to pray. Sometimes they say that one must have a special character, a religious predisposition, and a certain specific sensitivity in order to pray. They say, "Not everyone has this character and this sensitivity." But disciples who do not pray are disciples who listen little and are not able to listen to and turn to the Master.

Jesus realized that sometimes his disciples' actions were lacking the strength of heart that comes from prayer. In this regard there is a clear episode told in both the Gospels of Matthew and Mark. The disciples had not been able to help an epileptic child who was very ill. The father of the child went to Jesus to ask for help, adding that the disciples had not been able to do anything. Jesus, in turn, successfully healed the child. Afterward, the disciples "came to Jesus privately and said, 'Why could we not cast [the demon causing the epilepsy] out?' He said to them, 'Because of your little faith'" (Mt 17:19–20). In Mark's version, he tells the disciples, "This kind can come out only through prayer" (Mk 9:29). One needs faith to love the people, to love the poor. Faith manifests itself and grows through prayer. Through this episode, Jesus taught his disciples to understand the power of faith when dealing with a difficult case. He states, "if you have faith the size of a mustard seed, you will say to this mountain, 'Move from here to there,' and it will move; and nothing will be impossible for you" (Mt 17:20). Faith can move mountains. *Faith can do things that appear impossible.* Faith grows by listening to the word of the Lord and through prayer.

The Community of Sant'Egidio gathers to pray and to hear the word of the Lord. Jesus said to his people, "If two of you agree on earth about anything you ask, it will be done for you by my Father in heaven" (Mt 18:19). Many of Jesus' words in the Gospels teach us that prayer, made with faith and insistence, can accomplish much more than the work of our own hands—God listens to the prayer of his disciples. *The small community is not an abandoned and lonely group that lives in the forgotten corners of the world.* It is not an orphaned community. The Lord accompanies the community and listens to it, as a father listens to the voices of his sons and daughters, answering their requests, even if the children are immature. Moreover, Jesus, on many occasions, invites his disciples to ask with faith:

> Ask, and it will be given you; search, and you will find; knock, and the door will be opened for you. For everyone who asks receives, and everyone who searches finds, and for everyone who knocks, the door will be opened. Is there anyone among you

who, if your child asks for bread, will give a stone?
Or if the child asks for a fish, will give a snake? If
you then, who are evil, know how to give good gifts
to your children, how much more will your Father
in heaven give good things to those who ask him!
(Mt 7:7–11)

In both the prayer of community and in personal
prayer, the disciple believes in the power of faith. It is
something that does not appear powerful. It is a "weak
power." But faith moves the mountains. Even if the world
does not recognize the power of faith, we believe that
prayer and faith are strong. The Lord is not insensitive to
the requests of his disciples, like people, even people who
hold positions of responsibility, often are. Jesus teaches the
community to be insistent in prayer. The Lord does not get
tired of a persistent prayer. This is why Sant'Egidio gathers
many times during the week to pray together, to present
to the Lord the needs of the poor, the pain of countries
at war, the situations of the sister communities, and of all
Christians scattered throughout the world.

Every brother and sister of the community is called
on to read the scriptures personally, dwelling upon their
pages, especially the Gospels. It is in these pages that the
Lord speaks to us. From these pages, and from the preaching and the prayer of the community, we learn to address
the Lord. Indeed, each one of us, with all simplicity, can
address the Lord in prayer. The Lord listens to the little

ones. In the Psalms, we see how prayer is confidence in the Lord: "Hear, O Lord, when I cry aloud, be gracious to me and answer me!" (Ps 27). Jesus teaches us to address the Lord intimately: "Whenever you pray, go into your room and shut the door and pray to your Father who is in secret; and your Father who sees in secret will reward you" (Mt 6:6). Addressing the Lord with the weak strength of prayer, the community knows he will answer.

The Community that Gathers

The community gathers as a family around the Lord. It gathers to pray but also to listen. Prayer is often born from listening to the word of God. When attempting to pray, we often find ourselves unsure of what to say to God. The language of prayer can be learned by listening to the word of God and from the liturgy. For example, the Psalms suggest to us the words with which to address the Lord. At other times the chants and the hymns of the community may guide our prayer. *The Bible is in the very heart of the prayer meetings of the community.* It is the precious and holy book with which the Lord speaks to the community. The Gospels are a light that enlightens all the parts of the Bible.

The Bible is read at every prayer gathering of the community. Thus we listen to the word of the Lord. We must never get tired of listening to his word or of reading the pages of scripture. We must not say: "I know them already," or "I heard them before." We do not consume and throw away the book of the scriptures, the Bible, as we often do with many things in our life. The word of God grows with us during the years while we read it. As the years pass, we hear and understand the word better than we heard it and understood it in the past. It is the Lord who speaks to us. We must always pay great attention to the word of God and to the preaching that accompanies it. The apostle Paul teaches, "So faith comes from what is heard, and what is heard comes through the word of Christ" (Rom 10:17). This is why the community gathers together around the word of God. When the community gathers, the Bible must always be placed at the center of the meeting.

Every Community of Sant'Egidio is steadfast in prayer: it gathers to hear the word of the Lord, it sings his praise, it addresses to him its invocations. When the community gathers to pray, it hears what the Lord says to his disciples: "Come away to a deserted place all by yourselves and rest a while" (Mark 6:31). The true image of the community is that of brothers and sisters who gather in prayer. It is the meeting of the community. Moreover, Church—*ecclesia* in Greek—means assembly: the community meeting as one.

The place where the community gathers for prayer should always be carefully chosen. Whether the meeting takes place in a church or in another place appropriate for community prayer, care for the place chosen is important as it is the house of the family of the Lord. There should always be a Bible present, but besides the Bible, it is important to have an icon or an image of the Lord. Everyone can thus turn to the Lord's face and orient their prayer towards him. Psalm 27 reads, "'Come,' my heart says, 'seek his face!' Your face, Lord, do I seek. Do not hide your face from me." Moreover, it is meaningful to have some lights present, to show that the Lord is our light. Psalm 27 says, "The Lord is my light and my salvation; whom shall I fear?" As often as possible, the Easter candle should be lit at prayer, a sign of the risen Lord.

What occurs in the Gospels occurs in the community: "The apostles gathered around Jesus, and told him all that they had done and taught" (Mk 6:30). This happens in the meeting and prayer of the community. We speak to the Lord and he speaks to us. The meeting of the community is an important moment—it is the family gathering together. The community especially needs to pray, and to look one another in the face; to talk with one another, to exchange experiences, to understand together the path we are walking.

Ignatius of Antioch wrote, "If someone does not take part in the meeting of the faithful, he is an arrogant one who has already judged himself." During a particularly difficult time of persecution, he went on to say, "When you meet, the forces of Satan crumble, and his whips dissolve in the harmony taught by faith" (*Letter to the Ephesians* 5:3, 13). The gathering of the community brings together those who have been rescued from the logic of evil; the prayer of the community is strong, and it liberates from evil.[16]

Ignatius, who had a long experience at the service of the Christian community, writes to the leaders of one of the communities: "The meetings should be more frequent: invite all one by one" (*Letter to Polycarp* 4:2). All the meetings of the community, not only the prayer meetings, should be frequent, and each individual should feel personally invited. The community must not forget anyone. No one is merely a number in the community. The presence of each individual member is never unimportant.

We see in the scriptures as well how important these meetings are. They make charity grow. We read in the Letter to the Hebrews, "And let us consider how to provoke one another to love and good deeds, not neglecting to meet together, as is the habit of some, but encouraging one another" (Heb 10:24–25). The word and the presence of one another at the meeting exhort the community to be better, to be strengthened, and to find courage.

On the day of the Lord, the brothers and the sisters take part in the Eucharist, recognizing that Jesus is the Master and Lord of their lives. In the Eucharist, they pray for all the communities and for the whole Church. They receive the gift of eating his body and drinking from his cup; they draw from it the strength to continue their way toward the day when he will return. In fact, every Sunday is a gift to the community, a day to understand that its strength comes completely from the Lord, and not from its own hands.

The Community among the People: The Poor

The community does not live for itself, just as the disciples did not live for themselves. The community lives among the people and strives to do so with love. Among the disciples, there is a gift that grows with time: that gift is love. Often we do not realize this because we live within the reality of this love and take it for granted. But its existence is a decisive fact, both for the community and in the life of each disciple. It is the love between the brothers and sisters. It is the love and the care with which we look at all the others who are not part of the community. It is the love with which we look at the poor. It is the love with which we follow the life of the far-away peoples.

Love characterizes the community to those who view it from the outside. Jesus said, "Just as I have loved you, you also should love one another. By this everyone will know that you are my disciples, if you have love for one another" (Jn 13:34–35). Love shows that the disciples of Jesus are present. Some people may not like the disciples. Others will say bad things about them. Others still may tolerate or even grow to like them. But it is love that defines the community itself.[17] Love is not a one-time feeling, but a concrete way of living that we are to engage in every day.

For disciples who embrace this way of living, the first concern is with the poor. The poor are not an important reality for a society that normally pushes them to the margin; they have nothing to give back in return. The poor have neither riches to help us in the moment of need nor acquaintances who could introduce us to someone important. They are not the most cultivated of persons. So, why are they important for Christians?

One day John the Baptist, who was in jail, sent two of his disciples to Jesus to ask him if he was the Messiah or if they should wait for another. Jesus did not answer directly, but he invited the two disciples to look around and to see and hear what was happening. He said:

> Go and tell John what you hear and see: the blind receive their sight, the lame walk, the lepers are cleansed, the deaf hear, the dead are raised, and the poor have good news brought to them. And blessed is anyone who takes no offense at me. (Mt 11:4–7)

Jesus invites John's disciples to take a look around. Those who suffer are healed. The poor finally receive the good news: They are cared for. They are healed. Those who are wounded by life are also healed. The good news is preached. These things show the presence of the Lord among humanity. Love for the poor reveals the presence of the Lord, and love for the poor reveals the heart of the community. The community treasures the words of John XXIII, before the opening of the Second Vatican Council, when he invited the Church to be "the Church of all and especially of the poor."

The community may not be able to perform those great miracles that the disciples of John saw performed by Jesus.[18] But it can perform important signs that reveal the Lord is still in our midst. Maybe, even today, people such as those disciples of John could see the presence of the Gospel because the poor are loved and healed. There are still men and women who care for the poor: the sick, the children that are not helped by anyone, the old people who are often marginalized, the lepers of our own time, foreigners, people with difficulties, those who are shunned by everyone, lonely people, those who have suffered the violent wounds of life, prisoners.

People on the margins do not have much to give back in return. But the disciples care for them not because they may gain something. The poor are not powerful friends who can help them. But in every poor man or woman, the disciples see a brother and a sister of theirs. This is why they help them and care for them. And in this, the poor do indeed receive the good news: someone cares for them and considers them brothers and sisters! These people, who for much of society are irrelevant, are, on the contrary, very important to the community.

The poor are so important that men and women will be judged for their attitude toward them. The parable of the final judgment (Mt 25:31–46) reveals that whatever has been done to the poor has been done to the Lord himself, but whatever has been denied the poor has been denied the Lord himself. In fact, on the day of the judgment, the Lord will say to some people, "Come, you that are blessed by my Father, inherit the kingdom . . ." Why blessed? Jesus explains, "I was hungry and you gave me food, I was thirsty and you gave me something to drink, I was a stranger and you welcomed me, I was naked and you gave me clothing, I was sick and you took care of me, I was in prison and you visited me" (Mt 25:34–37). Those people are perplexed and ask, "when was it that we saw you hungry and gave you food, or thirsty and gave you something to drink? And when was it that we saw you a stranger and welcomed you, or naked and gave you clothing? And when was it that we saw you sick or in prison and visited you?" (Mt 25:37–39).

These questions are not only on the lips of those who are saved. They are also the questions of those who find themselves excluded from salvation because they have not given drink or food to the Lord, they have not welcomed him while in distress, and they have not visited him in need. They too, surprised, ask: "Lord, when was it that we saw you hungry or thirsty or a stranger or naked or sick or in prison, and did not take care of you?" (Mt 25:44). Jesus answers, "Truly, I tell you, just as you did not do it to one of the least of these, you did not do it to me" (Mt 25:45). *The poor are the little brothers and sisters of the Lord. Actually, the Lord goes so far as to identify himself with the poor.* In the pages of scripture, the Lord loves all who come to him but identifies only with the poor and with disciples who are persecuted. In fact, early in the Acts of the Apostles he says to Paul, "Saul, Saul, why do you persecute me?" (Acts 9:4).

The poor, the little ones of Jesus, are also the brothers and sisters of the community. They are our brothers and sisters, our relatives! The great Christmas lunch in the Basilica of Santa Maria in Trastevere in Rome that the Community prepares every year is the expression of this love for the poor that places them at the center of the community's life.[19] The poor are, in a very special way, part of the family of the community; they are its friends and the people for whom the community is responsible. *This is why wherever exists the Community of Sant'Egidio, there is also friendship with the poor.* Through this friendship, the poor receive the good news that they are considered friends and brothers and sisters.

As we see in the Gospel of Matthew's parable of the last judgment, and as James states in his letter, mercy covers many

Letter of James teaches the community to be a friend of the poor; we read, "What good is it, my brothers and sisters, if you say you have faith but do not have works? Can faith save you? If a brother or sister is naked and lacks daily food, and one of you says to them, 'Go in peace; keep warm and eat your fill,' and yet you do not supply their bodily needs, what is the good of that?"(Jas 2:14–16).

Love for the poor makes the faith of each disciple and of the entire community both genuine and ingenious. Ingenuity is necessary because, in today's world, the poor are many. There are many poor close to us, though sometimes we neither see them nor recognize them. But there are also poor who are far from us. We receive news and images of these distant poor. There are entire countries suffering from poverty or from war, which is the mother of all poverty. *The poor who are far away as well as those who are close are friends of the community.* The community tries not to forget them and, as it can, to help them.

The community's friendship with the poor teaches us that each one of us always has something to give—there is always some way to help. Jesus praises the small offering the widow puts in the temple treasury; he does not give much attention to the rich people who, with great display, put in a lot of money. Everyone can help the poor. *No one is so poor as not to be able to help someone.* Even if we experience difficulties, there is always someone poorer we can help. In the Acts of the Apostles, after Pentecost, Peter and John meet a lame man near the door of the temple in Jerusalem. He asks them for alms. The two apostles confess they have neither gold nor silver, but they give him what they have. Peter, in the name of Jesus, enables him to walk (Acts 3:1–10).

An ancient Christian text of the second century, known as the *Letter to Diognetus,* speaks about the poverty of the community of that time. As a matter of fact, there were few (if any) great or rich people in those first communities.[20] But the *Letter to Diognetus* states, "Christians are poor and enrich many." This is the beautiful praise that the brothers and sisters of the community must come to deserve today, in every part of the world.

The poor are the friends of the community; they are its relatives and its children, those for whom it cares. When a brother or a sister loves someone who has nothing to give in return, a small miracle occurs. On the one side, a hardened heart opens; on the other, a person in need is not abandoned in distress. The Letter of James considers the love for those who are weak a fundamental expression of Christian life: "Religion that is pure and undefiled before God, the Father," says the letter, is "to care for orphans and widows in their distress, and to keep oneself unstained by the world" (Jas 1:27).

FELLOWSHIP

The community is the family of those who have converted to the Lord and who listen to his word. This is why the disciples call themselves (and consider themselves) brothers and sisters. The apostle Paul writes to the community of Ephesus: "So then you are no longer strangers and aliens, but you are citizens with the saints and also members of the household of God" (Eph 2:19). The disciples are foreigners or strangers by birth. They do not have much in common. Sometimes they belong to different linguistic, national, or ethnic groups. But they do not remain strangers; they become brothers and sisters. It is very powerful to see this idea, written many centuries ago to the community of Ephesus, become true again today in so many parts of the world. The brothers and sisters are no longer strangers to one another. Their link to one another is no

ccidental or temporary, as if they were merely fel-
sts at an event.

Christians, Paul goes on in the Letter to the Ephesians,
are "built upon the foundation of the apostles and prophets, Christ Jesus himself as the cornerstone" (Eph 2:20).
Jesus speaks of the disciples as his family: "Whoever does
the will of God is my brother and sister and mother" (Mk
3:35). The meeting of the community, that is, the moment
in which the family that was scattered gathers, makes this
statement of Jesus come true as well as the common prayer,
when the brothers and the sisters recognize that they are
part of the same family that has only one Father and only
one Master.

Fellowship is expressed in the relationship between the
different communities as well. Even if they live in faraway
countries, they feel united by a profound link of kinship
as "fellow citizens with the saints." In the letters of the
apostles, the "saints" are first of all the disciples, that is, the
brothers and sisters of the community. For this reason, Paul
addresses his letters, for example, "to the saints who are in
Ephesus" (Eph 1:1). The communities of Sant'Egidio are
a family of different communities throughout the world,
where all are fellow citizens of the others. Sant'Egidio's first
community, the mother community in Rome, is linked to
all the other communities. The communities of the south
of the world are linked to those of the north, and they all
live the belief that there is a common destiny. The brothers
and sisters who live in the richer countries and the brothers

and sisters who live in less-developed countries are not separated. The kinship between these communities knows no boundary or distance. In this world where boundaries divide deeply and sometimes become walls, communion makes us close one to the other, and it makes us feel part of the same history.

In the community people become fellow citizens with one another, even if they do not have the same national citizenship. *The secret of this common citizenship is intimacy with God.* The history of the communities of Sant'Egidio, scattered in many parts of the world, is that of brothers and sisters who belong to different cultures and nations but who feel they belong to the same family of God. The life of one is important to the others, even if they live at a distance or do not speak the same language. This Christian kinship witnesses that all men and women belong to one great family. All men and women of the world, all the peoples, are in fact called to feel as if they were one family. This is the revelation of the Gospel: being brothers and sisters, having a common destiny notwithstanding differences, and feeling solidarity with one another. This is the experience of the Community of Sant'Egidio. A Christian community is a tree that grows in many different soils, because it is founded on the word of God and rooted in charity.

The brothers and sisters are required to behave as brothers and sisters in their daily lives. They are, first, jointly responsible for the proclamation of the Gospel, for service to the poor, for the life of the community. Ignatius of Antioch exhorts the disciples to live in this way: "Toil together, struggle together, run, suffer, sleep, wake up all together, as administrators of the things of God, as assistants and servants of his" (*Letter to Polycarp* 6:1). These were words written by Ignatius while he was being led prisoner toward martyrdom. The words resound like a testament, entrusted to the life of the community, to carry on the Gospel of the Lord. The brothers and sisters are called to toil and struggle together. *The communion and the solidarity between the brothers and sisters are the best organization for the work of the community.*

During the course of his ministry, the apostle Paul wrote to the community in Philippi. The brothers and sisters of Philippi worked hard for the sake of the Gospel, but Paul gave them some advice that is very relevant for our communities as well: "Do nothing from selfish ambition or conceit, but in humility regard others as better than yourselves. Let each of you look not to your own interests, but to the interests of others" (Phil 2:3–4). When rivalry or vainglory arise in the life of the community, one nearly ends up considering oneself superior to or better than others. We must not surrender to pride in the things we do, thus despising others or mistreating them.

We can see the dangers involved when working for the Gospel in the house of Mary and Martha, when Martha turns angrily to Mary because Martha was the one who worked while Mary was seated at the feet of Jesus listening

to his word. Martha is so much taken by her work
ends up rebuking Jesus himself: "Lord, do you
that my sister has left me to do all the work by myself?"
(Lk 10:40). We have to reflect on the answer Jesus gives to
Martha, in order to free ourselves from any spirit of rivalry:
"Martha, Martha, you are worried and distracted by many
things; there is need of only one thing. Mary has chosen
the better part, which will not be taken away from her"
(Lk 10:41–42).

*The work of the community always begins and ends with
the "better part" of Mary, that is, being seated at the Lord's
feet and listening to his word.* This is why the community's
common prayer often concludes the day, so as to remind
us that "there is need of only one thing." The prayer of the
evening is the "better part" of Mary. The disciple is not he
or she who is anxious and troubled about many things,
thus tempted to feel superior to everyone else: "Let each
of you," says the apostle Paul, "regard others as better than
yourselves," and "look not to your own interests but to the
interests of others" (Phil 2:3–4).

In their relationships and in their collaboration, the
brothers and sisters must not follow the habits of groups
and of families that judge one another and argue among
themselves to the point of bickering. "But not so with
you," says the Lord to the disciples who were discussing
who could be considered the greatest. The greatest in the
community—as the Lord teaches—is he who serves (Lk
22:26).

Among the brothers and sisters, there are people who are responsible for the community or for some aspect of its life. Their service nourishes familial bonds and recalls everyone to live his or her own responsibility. At the end of the First Letter to the Thessalonians, the apostle Paul asks the community: "But we appeal to you, brothers and sisters, to respect those who labor among you, and have charge of you in the Lord and admonish you; esteem them very highly in love because of their work" (1 Thess 5:12–13). The community must appreciate those who exercise responsibility. Every responsible person can listen as if the words that Paul writes to Timothy, who has been charged with the responsibility of a community, were addressed to him or her: "Pursue righteousness, godliness, faith, love, endurance, gentleness. Fight the good fight of the faith" (1 Tm 6:11–12). Service to the community through responsible leadership does not diminish but rather enlarges fellowship.

Daily life brings us many different situations, including burdens and difficulties. The love between the brothers and sisters is a sign of the presence and the love of the Lord within the community. This love must be a daily event, lived in the concreteness of everyday life either alone or with others. Within ordinary daily life among our fellows, each must consistently behave as a disciple of the Gospel. Sisters and brothers are called to help one another in good and bad health, in times of ease and in times of difficulty, one carrying the weight of the others.

Paul writes to the community of Corinth, where there were many difficult situations, including the occasional manifestation of mutual indifference. He states, "And if one member suffers, all suffer together with it" (1 Cor 12:26). The community is particularly called to stand by the brothers and sisters who are sick or in trouble. What this means in particular is that that all brothers and sisters of the community are called to suffer with those who are suffering. Paul adds: "You are the body of Christ and individually members of it" (1 Cor 12:27). To be the same body means to share the condition of each part: no part can be foreign to the rest of the body. In this respect, one part does not live on its own, but for the whole body. We often think that the best choice is to live for ourselves. This is a great illusion. Self-love, *filautia* in Greek, leads to life for oneself. In particular, it leads one to accumulate goods for oneself without feeling part of a common destiny in solidarity with those who need. The comparison between the body and the community that Paul makes in his writings explains very effectively the reality of being brothers and sisters in the community. We are not only collaborators, people with the same ideas, but a body that feels itself as such and considers the others as a part of itself.

The community is made of men and women of different cultures and social conditions; sometimes they are people of a different nationality or ethnic group. But no difference is stronger than our familial bond. Nothing can put anyone on the fringe of the community. In the common fellowship, what Paul writes to the Galatians becomes true. The Galatian community suffered from disputes born of social differences that existed within the community. In response, Paul states: "There is no longer Jew or Greek, there is no longer slave or free, there is no longer male and female; for all of you are one in Christ Jesus" (Gal 3:28).

The apostle Peter was a practicing Jew. But at the beginning of the life of the community—as is written in the Acts of the Apostles—he encountered the faith of a Roman centurion who asked to be baptized together with his pagan friends. Peter explained this experience, saying, "I truly understand that God shows no partiality" (Acts 10:34). The community binds different (and distant) people together. Christians become God's children! In the life of the community, in mutual respect and in love, the walls of division have been broken down.

Fellowship binds the disciples together as one single family. The poor become the friends of this family. This family radiates a spirit of kinship and kindness. Around the community, there are friends, collaborators, and admirers. Paul recommends to the Philippians: "Let your gentleness be known to everyone" (Phil 4:5). Friendship is the heart of the community's attitude toward everyone. It has no enemy, even if some may have shown it hostility. The community cultivates friendship toward everyone; it tries to encourage those who are depressed, and to support those who are tired; it talks with everybody, and it listens to everybody. Thus, the community tries to be like the Lord Jesus, who in the community's prayer is called "the friend of the people."

The brothers and sisters must always love each other, as the Lord ordered them. This love keeps the community pure. The brothers and sisters are called to honor one another: "outdo one another in showing honor," says Paul in the Letter to the Romans (Rom 12:10). Each one must always honor the other. The apostle adds some words that can be a true rule for the life of the community in the world:

> Let love be genuine; hate what is evil, hold fast to what is good; love one another with mutual affection; outdo one another in showing honor. Do not lag in zeal, be ardent in spirit, serve the Lord. Rejoice in hope, be patient in suffering, persevere in prayer. Contribute to the needs of the saints; extend hospitality to strangers. Bless those who persecute you; bless and do not curse them. Rejoice with those who rejoice, weep with those who weep. Live in harmony with one another; do not be haughty, but associate with the lowly; do not claim to be wiser than you are. Do not repay anyone evil for evil, but take thought for what is noble in the sight of all. If it is possible, so far as it depends on you, live peaceably with all. Beloved, never avenge yourselves, but leave room for the wrath of God; for it is written,

"Vengeance is mine, I will repay, says the Lord." No, "if your enemies are hungry, feed them; if they are thirsty, give them something to drink; for by doing this you will heap burning coals on their heads." Do not be overcome by evil, but overcome evil with good. (Rom 12:9–21)

SEEDS OF COMMUNION

The words of the apostle Paul that were addressed to the Christians of Rome were addressed to a community that, like many other early communities, lived with difficulties and, at times, suffered from intense persecution. Both then and today, brothers and sisters may feel that evil may be stronger than they thought—even in not-so-hard situations. In the end, they may think that love is not the best way to grant everybody a comfortable life; rather, this may appear a tragic naiveté. Other times, when they see the poor (whole countries sometimes) undergoing great pain, they may begin to become truly convinced that evil is stronger. Brothers and sisters can become tempted by discouragement. But they may also be tempted by aggression. As we see in Paul's Letter to the Romans: "Never avenge yourselves, but leave it to the wrath of God. . . . Do not be overcome by evil, but overcome evil with good" (Rom 12:17–21).

The community can never choose the ways of aggressiveness, of violence—of evil. Doing so would never produce victory. Rather, it would make for a serious defeat. The community must not be afraid of its own weakness. To deal with uncomfortable feelings of weakness, one often looks to force and material security; but, as the Gospel says, life does not depend on the goods one possesses. Therefore, the disciples must constantly look to their Master and not at the models of the world. Jesus, their Master, said: "Learn from me; for I am gentle and humble in heart" (Mt 11:29).

The word of God helps us to lift our eyes from our own feelings and thoughts and to look instead at the crucified Lord. The crucified Lord reveals that God has chosen neither strength nor power to be present in the world, but that he has chosen the weakness of Jesus of Nazareth. In the Letter to the Philippians we read that Jesus "emptied himself, taking the form of a slave, being born in human likeness. And being found in human form, he humbled himself and became obedient to the point of death—even death on a cross. Therefore God also highly exalted him, and gave him the name that is above every name" (Phil 2:7–9).

In his humiliation and death, Jesus is abandoned by his disciples. In fact—as we see in the passion narratives of the four Gospels—the disciples at first did not even understand the true extent to which Jesus humbled himself, who gave himself up into the hands of those who wanted to kill him without either defending himself or running away. He himself rebuked the disciple who, having been overcome by aggressiveness, had drawn the sword to defend him: "All who take the sword will perish by the sword" (Mt 26:52). Aggressiveness is not Jesus' choice, even in the moment of deadly danger and of highest risk, that of his own life. He doesn't accept the logic of either arms or escape in order to save himself.

Jesus lets Judas, his betrayer, kiss him; he also calls him "friend" and does not insult him as, it might seem to us, he deserved. Seeing the defenseless attitude of Jesus, his disciples, who had followed him from Galilee, fled. Perhaps they wanted to save their lives. They had the feeling that a terrible conspiracy had killed Jesus' dream. All those armed people, all the country's political and religious authorities, were now against him. What more could be done? The Master, with his beautiful dreams and his Gospel, had been defeated. His disciples fled when that dream seemed destroyed by the blows of force. Even Simon Peter, who had been chosen as the leader of that group, denied being one of his friends.

Every year during Holy Week, Christians remember that defeat. Every year they remember that dream defeated by force. The Cross of Jesus is a living memory of a tragic moment. The apostle Paul, in his preaching, began from the living memory of the crucified Lord, as he writes in the

First Letter to the Corinthians. He writes to a community where the brothers and sisters were lost in many discussions and lofty speeches: "For I decided to know nothing among you except Jesus Christ, and him crucified" (1 Cor 2:2). *Every time Christians celebrate the Eucharist, they call to mind the death of the crucified Lord.* For Christians, the memory of the passion and death of Jesus does not fade away, nor is it forgotten. It was a defeat in the eyes of the world and of his disciples. *But God did not abandon his Son in the grave.* The grave was not his last home on earth.

The angels say to the frightened women who went to the tomb on the first day of the week, on Sunday: "Why do you look for the living among the dead? He is not here, but has risen" (Lk 24:5). God did not abandon his Son to the grave but raised him from the dead. He appeared to Simon Peter and to the other apostles, then to some brothers. Jesus, risen from the dead, spoke with them, took a meal with them, invited them to preach the Gospel. *His last home on earth was the community of the disciples. That community is still his home.*

The resurrection of Jesus clearly shows that the way of humility does not end in death or in the grave but leads to life. Easter shows, as Paul says to the Ephesians:

> The immeasurable greatness of his power for us who believe, according to the working of his great power. God put this power to work in Christ when he raised him from the dead and seated him at his

> right hand in the heavenly places, far above all rule
> and authority and power and dominion, and above
> every name that is named, not only in this age but
> also in the age to come. (Eph 1:19–21)

The risen Jesus has gone through the way of humiliation and of the Cross, and, when he appears to the disciples, he still carries the wounds of that terrible death. But death was not the end of his dream. After his death, he still speaks to his friends. On the day of the Lord, the church celebrates Jesus' resurrection, remembering God's love for his humble Son, offered in redemption for many.

The community always remembers the death on the Cross of the Lord Jesus and his resurrection. It remembers thus the great love of the Master for his disciples, and for all. He did not aim to save his life above anything else. He could have saved himself, abandoning them and leaving Jerusalem—as the Gospels testify, he was aware of the conspiracy against him. But he remained. Moreover, as we read in the scriptures, he offered himself. The Son did not abandon his friends. God did not abandon his Son. *In the resurrection, all the love of the Father for the Son shines through.*

The community remembers Jesus' weakness; Jesus did not have powerful people on his side. He, who had benefited so many people, died alone, abandoned and humiliated—a poor man, as a person who had been condemned as a criminal. It is from this Master that the community learns not to be afraid of weakness, of its poor means, of small numbers, of difficulty, of poverty. It is from this Master that the community learns not to be tempted by violence or aggressiveness. It learns how not to desire riches or security to guarantee its life. The greatest guarantee is the love of God for his little disciples in the world: "for the Father himself loves you," says Jesus to his people at the moment of the farewell, just before his passion, "because you have loved me and have believed that I came from God" (Jn 16:27).

God does not dwell upon strength or riches. God looked faithfully upon the weakness of the Son and raised him from the dead. Paul then can say: "God chose what is foolish in the world to shame the wise" (1 Cor 1:27). This is why God loves his little disciples in the world. Fear, the awareness of one's own weakness, and discouragement when facing difficulties are very common human feelings. We may experience these feelings, but they are not the last word in our lives. We must not be dominated by fear, for fear is a wicked counselor. No amount of human strength is ever enough to reassure us in our fears, largely because human life is so frail. The first thing the risen Christ says to his disciples, who had shut their doors for fear, is: "Do not be afraid" (Mt 28:5–10). To overcome fear means to discover, both through faith and through concrete experience, that there is a great strength in the weak life of the Christian community.

Many times human strength is founded on evil. Other times it is based on arrogance. Other times, it is used to hide fear. But there is a strength that ripens in the "weakness" of faith, of love, of friendship, of prayer. It is a "weak strength." Paul was a man who had experienced weakness, persecution, hostility, imprisonment, and difficulties. He knew well what weakness was. But he strongly states "whenever I am weak, then I am strong" (2 Cor 12:10). The disciple discovers within his own weakness the "weak strength" of the Christian.

The instruments and means of this "weak strength" are not money, arrogance, overbearing manners, power, riches. Rather, they are love, prayer, fraternity, friendship, meekness, and compassion. Every community, small or large, must work with these evangelical instruments: it is in fact certain that the Lord will come and support them in their weakness. In this sense the Community is truly a gift of communion and love to the place where it lives, despite its being small and fragile. They believe that good will prevail over evil, love over hatred, truth over falsehood, peace over war. In order to accomplish this evangelical mission, it is necessary that the brothers and sisters be clothed in evangelical feelings and attitudes, without fear of amending or improving themselves.

The brothers and sisters who live according to the Gospel, who love and speak in heartfelt ways, are the community's strength. The strength of the community is its prayer to the Lord. The strength of the community is its union with the other communities all over the world. The strength of the community is listening to the Lord and learning from him who is gentle and humble. Jesus relies completely on the "weak strength" of faith and love. Just before his passion, after having talked for a long time with his disciples, Jesus says: "I have said this to you, so that in me you may have peace. In the world you face persecution, but take courage; I have conquered the world!" (Jn 16:33).

THE STORM

Life can be challenging for everyone. Our societies face divisions and unfairness. Sometimes the community itself can be shaken, both because of the situation in which it lives, or because of the individual condition of a brother or a sister. It happened to the first disciples, and it happens wherever there is Christian life. The Gospel guides us in dealing with the difficult situations that life can present.

In the Gospel of Matthew (Mt 8:23–27) we read that Jesus was once on a boat together with his disciples. A violent storm arose and it seemed that the boat was about to sink. Everybody was scared. The Lord seemed to be absent, for he was sleeping. They feared he was indifferent to their difficulties. So they started to cry out. They turned to the Lord and said, "Lord save us! we are perishing!" And he said to them, "Why are you afraid, you of little faith?"

Oftentimes fear comes from little faith. Jesus listens to the invocation his friends address to him in fear. He stood up and rebuked the winds and the sea. Then, as we read in Matthew's Gospel, the disciples were amazed. *Amazement is stronger than fear.* There is amazement among the family of the communities of Sant'Egidio: communities that are like many boats sailing on a sometimes stormy sea, and yet there is amazement when faith dissolves the fears of the brothers and sisters. There is amazement when many women and men learn how to love others. There is amazement when illness and marginalization that seemed impossible to change find healing, and when renewed human coexistence arises. There is amazement that the boat of the community can sail on so many different seas, can cross the barriers of separation, and can reach peoples distant from one another. *The Lord is stronger than any storm, whether the storm comes from the outside, or is one that arises in the heart of any of us.* There are, in fact, serious storms of the heart. St. Paul says:

> Do not worry about anything, but in everything by prayer and supplication with thanksgiving let your requests be made known to God. And the peace of God, which surpasses all understanding, will guard your hearts and your minds in Christ Jesus. (Phil 4:6–7)

The Lord speaks, and the storm calms. Be anxious for nothing, but let your requests be made known to God, for he guards our hearts and minds! The Lord is stronger than any storm that might arise in our communities. We trust the Lord. We read in the Letter of Peter, "Humble yourselves therefore under the mighty hand of God, so that he may exalt you in due time. Cast all your anxiety on him, because he cares for you" (1 Pt 5:6–7).

The words of Jesus calm any storm. It is truly amazing that a word can be so concrete and so effective. The word of God is able to give birth to and nurture a life that is able to open hearts, defeat violence, produce generosity and love. God so loved men and women that he came to dwell among them.[21] This peace is not for the community alone. Like a city on top of a hill, the disciples of the Lord are called to share the Good News of the living Gospel.

Conclusion:

A Life for Everybody

～

What has been written so far is meant to outline some aspects of the life of the Community of Sant'Egidio. It is meant to show how the word of God generates and nurtures a new life, and to show how the word of God is not an obscure, difficult thing. The word of God is accessible—it is neither impossible to understand nor impossibly difficult to live out. True, not everything is clear, even when one is well on the way. Christian life is not something you learn by heart. It is life, in fact. When one lives as a disciple, one understands it better. Jesus, before leaving his disciples, said to them: "I still have many things to say to you, but you cannot bear them now. When the Spirit of truth comes, he will guide you into all the truth" (Jn 16:12–13).

The Spirit is leading us along the life of the community, into all truth. In community, we start to understand a few "things." The word of God grows as we listen to it and as we read it. Love grows as we walk on his path. Faith and love are stronger than our sin; they are stronger than the powers of this world, stronger than difficulties. Beyond the storms, we have met a great peace in the Lord and in his family. He said, "Peace I leave with you; my peace I give to you; I do not give to you as the world gives" (Jn 14:27). Yes, Jesus left with us a great peace, and we live it within his family! Let us then open up our lives to the Gospel. We are convinced that if we open up our hearts to the Gospel, the whole world will open up to love.

PART TWO

THE PRAYER

OF THE

COMMUNITY

"Lord, Teach Us to Pray"

Prayer is the heart of the the Community of Sant'Egidio and is its absolute priority. At the end of each day, every community of Sant'Egidio, large or small, gathers around the Lord to listen to his word. The word of God and the prayer are, in fact, the very basis of the community's life. The disciples cannot do other than remain at the feet of Jesus, as did Mary of Bethany, to receive his love and learn his ways, as Paul invites the disciples in the Letter to the Phlippians: "Let the same mind be in you that was in Christ Jesus" (Phil 2:5).

A key part of community prayer is the Bible, which is always placed in the center of the community's prayer space. Placing a bible prominently in the places of prayer reflects the centrality of the word of God both for our prayer and our lives. The Bible is the precious book that we listen to over and over, not growing tired of it, but rather growing into it, as Pope Gregory the Great wrote. The daily readings taken both from the Old and New Testament follow usually the *Lectio Divina* and the lectionary of the Catholic Church for the Sunday liturgy.

Many of the community's prayers include the psalms. The psalms have always been part of the prayer of the community. They are sung as part of the Prayer for the Poor, the Prayer of the Mother of God, and the Prayer of the Church. Jesus knew the psalms by heart, and prayed with them frequently, even on the Cross. The Book of the Psalms is the Bible book devoted to prayer—it nourishes both our personal and communal prayer. Dietrich Bonhoeffer wrote: "Thus if the Bible also contains a prayerbook, we learn from this that not only that Word which he has to say to us belongs to the Word of God, but also that word which he wants to hear from us" (*Psalms: The Prayer Book of the Bible*). The Psalter teaches us the words we can and we should say to God. In praying with the psalms we form our first relationship with God. This is why the Psalter is so important to the community's prayer. With it, we enter into relationship with God and move toward true wisdom.

In the 1990s, the community began using the icon of the face of Jesus in its prayer. The icon communicates a true beauty, one different from the alluring but often fake beauties of our world. The beauty of this icon, which comes from the Ukraine and may date to the sixteenth or seventeenth century (the original of which is kept in the

Church of Sant'Egidio), connects us with much history and with much suffering. The icon of the face of Jesus speaks to how the Lord loves each of us. Meditated on in faith, it says to the heart of each of us, "Seek his face! Do not hide your face from me" (Ps 27).

Another key component in Sant'Egidio's community prayer is the lighting of the paschal candle. It reminds us of Easter and symbolizes Jesus' life—risen and alive for and in us. The community also cultivates the living beauty of singing during prayer, which, like incense, perfumes the places where we pray. Singing is an important ministry in the community, and much time is devoted to making this singing prayerful.

Lastly, it is very important that the places of prayer be welcoming places that present not just a public space, but a house and home. You do not enter someone's home anonymously. Any home worthy of the name offers welcome, introduction, and, hopefully, memory. The community always tries to remember those who have attended the prayer. This expression of welcome and memory stands in contrast with the sad experience of anonymity that so often marks life in today's cities.

So every evening, when the community returns to the feet of the Lord, it repeats the words of the anonymous disciple: "Lord, teach us to pray." Jesus, Master of prayer, continues to answer: "When you pray, say: Father" (Lk 11:1–2). This is not a simple exhortation, it is much more. With these words, Jesus lets the disciples participate in his own relationship with the Father. Therefore, in prayer, the fact of being children of the Father who is in heaven comes before whatever words we may say. Praying is, above all, a way of being! That is to say, we are children who turn with faith to the Father, certain that we will be heard.

Jesus teaches us to call God "our Father," and not simply "Father" or "my Father." Even when they pray on their own, disciples are never isolated, nor are they orphans: they are always members of the Lord's family. In praying together, besides the mystery of being children of God, there is also the mystery of fraternity. As Saint Cyprian of Carthage, a father of the Church, said: "You cannot have God as father without having the church as mother." (*Treatise on Unity* 6). When praying together, the Holy Spirit assembles the disciples in the upper room together with Mary, the Lord's mother, so that they may direct their gaze toward the Lord's face and learn from Him the secret of his heart.

The communities of Sant'Egidio all over the world gather in the various places of prayer and lay before the Lord the hopes and sufferings of the tired, exhausted crowds of whom the Gospel speaks. In these ancient crowds we see the huge masses of modern cities: the millions of refugees who continue to flee their countries; the poor, relegated to the very fringe of life; and all those who are waiting for someone to take care of them. Praying together includes the cry, the invocation, the aspiration, the desire for peace, the healing and salvation of the men and women of the world. Prayer is never in vain; it rises ceaselessly to the Lord, so that anguish is turned into hope, tears into joy, despair into happiness, and loneliness into communion. May the kingdom of God come soon among people!

Toward the Day of the Lord

It is easy for the hectic rhythms and the frantic deadlines of life to make us organize our time without reference to the Lord. Even Jesus, in the desert, was tempted by the devil, who wanted to distract him from the Father and from his mission. With the word of God, Jesus subdues the devil. The word of God announced every evening descends upon the disciples because, by gazing at the face of Jesus, they can imitate him in their lives. The weekly rhythm, taken as a measure of time in the common prayer of the Community of Sant'Egidio, manifests more clearly, in the convulsive life of the contemporary city, the orientation toward the Lord's day.

Therefore **Sunday** becomes the climax of the life of the community! The disciples meet the risen Lord. It is the day of Emmaus; after listening to the word of God, the breaking of the bread is celebrated and the eyes of the disciples are opened, and they recognize him. It is the weekly Easter, which announces the eternal Easter when God will prevail over evil and death for good.

On **Monday** the week's work begins. On this day, the community recognizes that the Lord's face has no longer the features of the risen Savior, but those of the poor, the weak, the sick, and the suffering. Monday's evening prayer remembers the poor, those encountered during the day and those far off, sometimes whole nations that suffer; all are presented to the Lord so that he will console them and free them from evil.

Mary, the Mother of God and first among believers, accompanies the community in the **Tuesday** prayer, so that everyone learns from her "to treasure all these things in the heart" (Lk 2:51) what we have heard and to thank the Lord because he has looked upon us poor men and women. The truth of the Lord's words, "What is impossible for mortals is possible for God" (Lk 18:27), has become a daily experience for the community.

The following day, **Wednesday**, the communities of Sant'Egidio scattered throughout the world pray for one another and for the whole Church. Everyone prays in the profound, outreaching, and joyful communion that the Lord bestows on his children; Wednesday's prayer embraces the saints, invoked by name, so that they accompany all the communities along the roads of the world.

On **Thursday** all the Churches, both of the east and of the west, are remembered so that communion among believers in Christ may increase and that the preaching of the Gospel reaches the ends of the earth. The Lord, the only pastor of his Church, bestows upon all his passionate love from which spring pastoral action and commitment to announcing the Gospel.

On **Fridays** the community focuses on the "memory of the Cross" so that everyone may remember the origin of salvation and not forget how great the love of God for humankind has been. The link between the beatitudes and the story of the passion leads us to contemplate the infinite "wealth" of the Cross, which is the proclamation both of the death of self-love and of the victory of love for others.

Then comes **Saturday**, the day of vigil and preparation for the Lord's resurrection. It is the waiting of Lazarus to be unbound. In him is heard the cry for help, which rises from every part of the earth, to be presented to the Lord, imploring the Lord to take away the heavy stone that oppresses life, the life of us all, freed from the bonds of sin and saved by God's mercy. Thus the week does not close in a casual or chaotic manner. The days guided by prayer are oriented toward the day that knows no sunset, when, together with the angels, the disciples will sing the Trisagion, or "Thrice Holy," which concludes the "Prayer of Light" of Sunday evening.

The community has crafted prayers for special days as well. The **Prayer of the Holy Spirit** reminds the community to open its heart to the breath of God so as to fight the spirits of evil and to increase the works of mercy upon earth; this prayer is used at Pentecost. On the feast days of the apostles, the community follows the **Prayer of the Apostles** in which they and their task of announcing the Gospel are remembered. This memory sustains and encourages the commitment of the community to follow the first witnesses of faith to the end of the earth. **The Prayers of Christmas and of Easter** are used in those liturgical times to stress the relevance of the celebrations. **The Prayer of the Sick** is used once a month with a special prayer of intercession for those who are sick.

Lastly, a word about icons: icons, present in every church of the community, introduce us to the riches of the spiritual tradition of the Eastern Church and help us to direct the eyes of our hearts toward the Lord and to place all our trust in Him.

THE WEAK STRENGTH OF PRAYER

Nothing is possible without prayer—all is possible with prayer and faith. With their lack of faith the people of Nazareth even prevented the Lord from working miracles (Lk 4:21–30). When they did not pray and fast, the disciples themselves were not able to cure people. Prayer overcomes human helplessness. It goes beyond what is believed impossible and allows God to intervene in this world with his inifinite power.

James writes in his letter: "You ask and do not receive, because you ask wrongly, in order to spend what you get on your pleasures" (Jas 4:3). While taking care of the poor and the weak, the community learns from them to turn to God with their trust and persistence, and each of us finds himself or herself a beggar for love and peace. Thus, with greater awareness, we can stretch out our hands to the Lord, and the Lord, gracious Father and friend of humankind, will answer with generosity beyond all expectations.

Prayer appears weak in the eyes of the world. But, when it is full of faith in the Lord, prayer is strong indeed. It can break down walls, fill voids, uproot violence, and increase mercy. Praying together is indeed holy and blessed; it is necessary for the life of every disciple and for the life of the community, but it is also necessary for the very life of the world. It is written, "if two of you agree on earth about anything you ask, it will be done for you by my Father in heaven" (Mt 18:19). That is why the disciple and the community must persevere and be audacious in common prayer. Prayer, in fact, is a powerful weapon in the hands of believers: it destroys evil and increases love.

In the Prayer of Sant'Egidio, the pleas of those near and far, of the poor and the weak, of our brothers and sisters, are united almost as though they are part of a "virtual" but real cathedral that gathers everyone in a single invocation to God. By praying together, we can make ours the words of the apostle Peter: "Come to him, a living stone, though rejected by mortals yet chosen and precious in God's sight, and like living stones, let yourselves be built into a spiritual house, to be a holy priesthood, to offer spiritual sacrifices acceptable to God through Jesus Christ" (1 Pt 2:4–5).

Prayer for the Days of the Week

Saturday: Prayer of the Vigil

Hymn

> Wanting to see the tomb of Lazarus, O Lord,
> you who prepared yourself for the grave,
> you asked, "Where have you placed him?"
> And you learnt what you already knew.
> You cried out to the one you loved,
> "Lazarus, come out!"
>
> He who had died obeyed you, O Lord,
> you who give life to all humanity.

It was the fourth day since he died, O Lord,
yet you came to his sealed tomb,
and shed your tears for Lazarus,
because your friend had died.

Blessed are you, O Lord,
friend of the people,
have mercy on us. (2 times)

Through your voice, death was bound up,
Lazarus was freed from the bonds of death.
At this sight, your disciples rejoiced
and their mouths filled with a festal song:
Blessed are you, O Lord, friend of the people,
have mercy on us.

Your voice, O Lord,
has destroyed death.
Your power heals those who are sick,
your word raises up the dead,
and Lazarus is the foretaste
of our salvation.

Blessed are you, O Lord . . . (2 times)

All things are possible to you, O Lord,
our good friend.
Pardon the sin of your servants,

spread your mercy over us,
heal, with your love,
all peoples so wounded.

Taking the disciples with you, O Lord,
and drawing close to the tomb of Lazarus,
you called him by name, to life anew;
you awakened him from his deep slumber;
he came out from the tomb at your word,
clothed in the fourth-day shroud
of death, and cried out.

Blessed are you, O Lord . . . (2 times)

Rejoice! Town of Bethany,
homeland of Lazarus.
Rejoice! Martha and Mary, his sisters,
tomorrow, the Christ will come to give us life.
He will unbind every person from their bondage
to death and to sin.

Blessed are you, O Lord . . . (2 times)

Reading of the Word of God

Alleluia, alleluia, alleluia
(*Lent*: Praise to you, O Lord, praise be to you.)
Whoever lives and believes in me
will never die.

Alleluia, alleluia, alleluia

Alleluia, alleluia, alleluia

If you believe, you will see the glory of God,
thus says the Lord.

Alleluia, alleluia, alleluia

Invocations

Sure of the mercy of God,
we pray to the Lord.

Have mercy, O Lord, have mercy, O Lord,
have mercy, O Lord.

May the Lord unbind us
    from the bondage of our sins
and recall us to true life.

Have mercy, O Lord, have mercy, O Lord,
have mercy, O Lord.

May the Lord deliver all
    from burdens oppressing them
and kindle in them new life.

Have mercy, O Lord, have mercy, O Lord,
have mercy, O Lord.

May the Lord hasten to save us
and all in our city.

Have mercy, O Lord, have mercy, O Lord,
have mercy, O Lord.

Sure of the mercy of the Lord,
let us open our hearts to him.

Have mercy, O Lord, have mercy, O Lord,
have mercy, O Lord.

Trisagion

Holy God, Holy Mighty,
  Holy Immortal, have mercy on us.

Holy God, Holy Mighty,
  Holy Immortal, have mercy on us.

Holy God, Holy Mighty,
  Holy Immortal, have mercy on us.

Glory to the Father, to the Son,
  and to the Holy Spirit,
unto ages of ages. Amen.

All-holy Trinity, have mercy on us.
Lord, accept the expiation of our sins.
Master, pardon our iniquities.
Holy One, protect us,

heal our infirmities.

Lord, have mercy.
Lord, have mercy.
Lord, have mercy.

Glory to the Father, to the Son, and to
    the Holy Spirit,
unto ages of ages. Amen.

Our Father

SUNDAY: PRAYER OF THE DAY OF THE LORD

Hymn of the Resurrection

Alleluia, alleluia, alleluia
    Christ is risen from the dead
    and will die no more.
Alleluia, alleluia, alleluia
(*Lent*: Praise to you, Lord Jesus
Christ, king of endless glory.)

Despite the tomb's heavy stone,
the sorrowful sin of this world,
the guards keeping watch over your body,
you are risen, Lord, our God.

Alleluia, alleluia, alleluia . . .

To the women who came to the tomb,
an angel spoke of your resurrection.
You became the disciples' companion,
and in Emmaus, you broke bread with them.

Alleluia, alleluia, alleluia . . .

Despite the closed doors and fear,
you appeared to the gathered disciples,
gave them power to forgive,
and offered them your peace.

Alleluia, alleluia, alleluia . . .

Today, throughout the world, with faith,
we celebrate your resurrection.
From the depths of our hearts we confess,
you are our Lord and our God.

Alleluia, alleluia, alleluia . . .

Song of the Light

Come, receive the light
  from the light that does not end.

Your resurrection has enlightened the world.
Come, receive the light
  from the light that does not end.

Darkness and death are put to flight.
Come, receive the light
  from the light that does not end.

Your day has no knowledge of night.
Come, receive the light
  from the light that does not end.

Your light enlightens your servants.
Come, receive the light
  from the light that does not end.

Your love guards your disciples.
Come, receive the light
    from the light that does not end.

Reading of the Word of God

Alleluia, alleluia, alleluia
(*Lent*: Praise to you, Lord Jesus Christ, king of
    endless glory.)

Yesterday I was buried with Christ,
today I rise with you who are risen.
With you I was crucified;
remember me, Lord, in your kingdom.

Alleluia, alleluia, alleluia

Responsorial Song

May our prayer rise like incense in your presence,
my uplifted hands like an evening sacrifice.

To you, O Lord, I lift up my eyes.
Today I believe, help my unbelief.

The man called Jesus healed me;
I was blind, and now I see.

To you, O Lord, I lift up my eyes.
Today I believe, help my unbelief.

May our prayer rise like incense in your presence,
my uplifted hands like an evening sacrifice.

Invocations

Kyrie eleison, Kyrie eleison, Kyrie eleison

Sunday Intercessions

Let us pray to the Lord
    in the light of his resurrection
with all the saints
who, today and through the centuries,
have proclaimed he is risen.

May our prayer rise like incense in your presence,
my uplifted hands like an evening sacrifice.

We pray to the Lord in the communion of his Spirit
with all his servants
who everywhere celebrate in thanksgiving.

May our prayer rise like incense in your presence,
my uplifted hands like an evening sacrifice.

Song to Mary

Rejoice, O Virgin, Mother of God,
Mary, full of grace, the Lord is with you.

For blessed are you among all women
and blessed is the fruit of your womb.

Because you have given birth to the Savior. (*3 times*)

(*alternatively*)

O do not weep, Mother of God,
beside the Cross of Christ, our Savior.
Be joyful, for truly he is risen;
in his body there lies hidden
all the ransom
and the salvation
of all people. (*3 times*)

Trisagion

Holy God, Holy Mighty,
Holy Immortal, have mercy on us.

Holy God, Holy Mighty,
Holy Immortal, have mercy on us.

Holy God, Holy Mighty,
Holy Immortal, have mercy on us.

Glory to the Father, to the Son,
    and to the Holy Spirit,
unto ages of ages. Amen.

All-holy Trinity, have mercy on us.
Lord, accept the expiation of our sins.
Master, pardon our iniquities.

Holy One, protect us,
heal our infirmities.

Lord, have mercy.
Lord, have mercy.
Lord, have mercy.

Glory to the Father, to the Son,
   and to the Holy Spirit,
unto ages of ages. Amen.

Our Father

MONDAY: PRAYER FOR THE POOR

Invitatory

O God, come to our assistance.
O Lord, make haste to help us.

Glory to the Father, and to the Son, and to
     the Holy Spirit,
now and forever. Amen. Alleluia.
(*Lent*: Praise be to you.)

Psalmody

Reading of the Word of God

Alleluia, alleluia, alleluia
(*Lent*: Praise to you, Lord Jesus Christ, king of
     endless glory.)

This is the Gospel of the poor,
liberation for the imprisoned,
sight for the blind,
freedom for the oppressed.

Alleluia, alleluia, alleluia

Alleluia, alleluia, alleluia
The Son of Man came to serve,
whoever wants to be great
should become servant of all.

Alleluia, alleluia, alleluia

Song of Intercession

O God, come to our assistance.

O Lord, make haste to help us.

Lord, you heard the lament
of your people in Egypt.

Receive the lament
of the oppressed and exiled people.

Make haste to help them
and they will be saved.

Lord, you healed the lepers
who presented themselves before you.

Heal the sick,
be near to those in need.

Make haste to help them
and they will be saved.

You delivered the possessed,
free those who are not masters of themselves.

Make haste to help them
and they will be saved.

You gave sight to the blind
and strength to the paralyzed.

Make everyone able
to see and communicate.

Make haste to help them
and they will be saved.

You called the dead back to life.
You restored them to the light.

Do not allow death to reign,
give back life to your servants.

Make haste to help them
and they will be saved.

You ate with the sinner
and forgave every sin.

Look at our misery and sorrow.
Forgive all our sins.

Come quickly to our help
and we will be saved.

For you are a good God
and a friend of the people.

Our Father

TUESDAY: PRAYER WITH MARY, MOTHER OF GOD

Invitatory

O God, come to our assistance.
O Lord, make haste to help us.

Glory to the Father, and to the Son,
    and to the Holy Spirit,
now and forever. Amen. Alleluia.
(*Lent*: Praise be to you.)

Hymn

"How is it possible to have a son
if I have never known a man,"
the troubled woman asks herself
at the words of the angel of God.

"How is it possible for a man
to be born again when he is old?"

Nicodemus demanded of Jesus,
"Can he go back into his mother's womb?"

"The Holy Spirit will come upon you,
the power of the Most High overshadow you.
You will give birth to a son.
You must give him the name of Jesus."

"He who is not born again of the Spirit
is not able to enter my kingdom.
As you feel the breath of the wind,
so you will hear the Spirit of the Father."

"How can all this be possible?"
"If you have faith all is possible."
The Mother of God, so blessed:
"Be it unto me according to your word."

Psalmody

Reading of the Word of God

Alleluia, alleluia, alleluia
(*Lent*: Praise to you, Lord Jesus Christ, king of
endless glory.)

The Spirit of the Lord is upon you.
The child you shall bear will be holy.

Alleluia, alleluia, alleluia

Alleluia, alleluia, alleluia
Look down, O Lord, on your servants.
Be it unto us according to your word.

Alleluia, alleluia, alleluia

Magnificat *(optional)*

My soul magnifies the Lord,
and my spirit rejoices in God, my Savior.

For he has looked on the humility of his servant.
From now on all generations will call me blessed;

for the Mighty One has done great things for me,
and holy is his name!

His mercy is for those who fear him
from generation to generation.

He has shown strength with his arm;
he has scattered the proud in the
        thoughts of their hearts.

He has brought down the powerful from
        their thrones,
and lifted up the lowly;

He has filled the hungry with good things,
and sent the rich away empty.

He has helped his servant Israel,
in remembrance of his mercy,

according to the promise he made to our ancestors,
to Abraham and his descendants forever.

My soul magnifies the Lord,
and my spirit rejoices in God, my Savior.

Song to Mary

Rejoice, O Virgin, Mother of God,
Mary, full of grace, the Lord is with you.

For blessed are you among all women
and blessed is the fruit of your womb.

Because you have given birth to the Savior. (*3 times*)

(*alternatively*)

O do not weep, Mother of God,
beside the Cross of Christ, our Savior.
Be joyful, for truly he is risen;
in his body there lies hidden
all the ransom
and the salvation
of all people. (*3 times*)

Our Father

WEDNESDAY: PRAYER WITH THE SAINTS

Hymn

The prayers of the saints of the earth
rise up to you, O gracious Lord,
and there they sing a new song
gathered in front of your throne.

No one is able to understand the song,
only those redeemed from the world,
who follow the Lamb on all his ways,
the first-fruits of God without stain.

You are worthy to take the scroll,
worthy to break its seals,
because you were sacrificed
and have redeemed us with your blood.

You have redeemed us, we of every language,
of every people, race, and nation,
you have made of us one people,
a people of priests and kings.

Holy, Holy, Holy
is the Lord God Almighty.
Who was, and is, and is to come,
who is worthy to receive all glory.

Responsorial Song

Salvation belongs to our God!

Amen. Praise, glory, and wisdom,
thanksgiving, honor, and power,
strength to our God from age to age.
Amen.

Ever-blessed is the Lord.
His saints will hunger no more.
Ever-blessed is the Lord.

His saints will thirst no more.
Ever-blessed is the Lord.

His saints will no longer be scorched by the sun.
Ever-blessed is the Lord.

The Lord will be their shepherd,
and will lead them to springs of the water of life.

He will wipe away all their tears
and death shall be no more.

Neither mourning, nor crying, nor pain.
Because the things of the past have gone.
Ever-blessed is the Lord. Amen.

Reading of the Word of God

Alleluia, alleluia, alleluia
(*Lent*: Praise to you, Lord Jesus Christ, king of
  endless glory.)

You are a chosen race,
a royal priesthood, a holy nation,
a people acquired by God
to proclaim his marvelous works.

Alleluia, alleluia, alleluia

Alleluia, alleluia, alleluia
You will be holy,
because I am holy, thus says the Lord.
Alleluia, alleluia, alleluia

Litany of the Saints

O Lord, have mercy on us all
    O Lord, have mercy on us all
O Christ, have mercy on us all
    O Christ, have mercy on us all
O Lord, have mercy on us all
    O Lord, have mercy on us all
Holy Mary, Mother of God,
    pray with us
Holy Mary of Mercy,
    pray with us

All you holy prophets,
    pray with us
Saint John the Baptist,
    pray with us
All you holy evangelists and apostles,
    pray with us
Holy disciples of the Lord,
    pray with us
Saints Peter and Paul,
    pray with us
Saint Andrew,
    pray with us
Saint James,
    pray with us
Saint Bartholomew,
    pray with us
Saint Mary of Magdala,
    pray with us
Saint Callistus,
    pray with us
Saint Cecilia,
    pray with us
Saint Anthony,
    pray with us
Saints Cosmas and Damian,
    pray with us
Saint Basil,
    pray with us

Saint John Chrysostom,
   pray with us
Saint Augustine,
   pray with us
Saint Benedict,
   pray with us
Saint Scholastica,
   pray with us
Saint Gregory,
   pray with us
Saint Giles,
   pray with us
Saints Cyril and Methodius,
   pray with us
Saint Adalbert,
   pray with us
Saint Francis,
   pray with us
Saint Clare,
   pray with us
Saint Frances of Rome,
   pray with us
Saint Philip Neri,
   pray with us
Holy bishops and pastors,
   pray with us
Holy monks and hermits,
   pray with us

Holy martyrs,
> pray with us

Holy virgins and widows,
> pray with us

All you who are poor in spirit,
> pray with us

All you who are weary and oppressed,
> pray with us

All you who thirst for justice,
> pray with us

All you people of goodwill,
> pray with us

All you saints of this city,
> pray with us

Brothers and sisters, wherever you may be,
> pray with us

Free us from sin and death,
> O Lord, hear our prayer

Free us from violence and injustice,
> O Lord, hear our prayer

Free us from loneliness and fear,
> O Lord, hear our prayer

Free us from all anxiety,
> O Lord, hear our prayer

Free us from every evil,
> O Lord, hear our prayer

Give us fullness of life,
> O Lord, hear our prayer

Give freedom to prisoners,
   O Lord, hear our prayer,
Give healing to the sick,
   O Lord, hear our prayer
Give peace to those who hinder us,
   O Lord, hear our prayer
Show us your holy face,
   and we shall be saved.

Our Father

Thursday: Prayer of the Church

Invitatory

O God, come to our assistance.
O Lord, make haste to help us.

Glory to the Father, and to the Son, and to
     the Holy Spirit,
now and forever. Amen. Alleluia.
(*Lent*: Praise be to you.)

Hymn

The gate is opened for the shepherd,
the sheep listen to his voice,
for he calls them one by one,
out of the fold he leads them.

The shepherd carefully guides them,
his sheep all follow him,
his voice is familiar to them,
they gather round when he calls them.

My sheep are astray and wander,
like sheep without a shepherd,
over mountains and hills,
with no one to seek or care for them.

My flock has become a prey,
its pasture has been trampled,
its water has been muddied,
hired hands have come instead.

Jesus says to the crowd he gathers:
"Truly I am the good shepherd,
I have come to take up my flock,
and all who listen to my voice.

"I lay down my life for my sheep,
so weak, and suffering, and lost.
Gathered in one fold together,
they will be the flock of one shepherd."

Psalmody

Reading of the Word of God

Alleluia, alleluia, alleluia
(*Lent*: Praise to you, Lord Jesus Christ, king of
   endless glory.)

I am the good shepherd,
my sheep listen to my voice,
and they become
one flock and one fold.
Alleluia, alleluia, alleluia

Alleluia, alleluia, alleluia
I give you a new commandment,
that you love one another.

Alleluia, alleluia, alleluia

Prayer of Intercession

Release my soul from prison
that I may praise your name.

Lord, receive our evening prayers,
grant us forgiveness for our sins,
because you showed the world
your glorious resurrection.

The just people are waiting
for you to fill them with your goodness.

Come, peoples, let us sing,
let us bow before the Lord,
let us joyfully glorify
his resurrection from the dead.

From the depths I cry to you, O Lord,
kindly listen to my prayer.

Come, peoples, let us sing,
let us bow before the Lord,
let us joyfully glorify
his resurrection from the dead.

Because he is our God
who frees the world
from loneliness and tears,
from the lie of the enemy.

Song of Zechariah *(optional)*

Blessed be the Lord, the God of Israel,
he has visited his people and redeemed them.

He has raised up for us a mighty savior
in the house of David his servant,
as he promised by the lips of holy men,
those who were his prophets from of old.

A savior who would free us from our foes,
from the hands of all who hate us.
So his love for our fathers is fulfilled
and his holy covenant remembered.

He swore to Abraham our father to grant us,
that free from fear, and saved from the hands
    of our foes,
we might serve him in holiness and justice,
all the days of our life in his presence.

As for you, little child,
you shall be called prophet of God, the Most High.
You shall go ahead of the Lord
to prepare his ways before him,

To make known to his people their salvation,
through the forgiveness of all their sins,
the loving kindness of our God,
who visits us like the dawn from on high.

He will give light to those in darkness,
those who dwell in the shadow of death,
and guide us into the way of peace.

Blessed be the Lord, the God of Israel,
he has visited his people and redeemed them.

Our Father

FRIDAY: PRAYER OF THE HOLY CROSS

Hymn

Standing near the Cross of the Lord
were his mother, Mary, and her sister,
Mary of Clopas, and Mary of Magdala.
Jesus looked on them with the beloved disciple.

Jesus said to his mother,
"O woman, this is your son,"
and to his disciple he said,
"This is your mother."

Blessed is the Lord alone on the Cross,
who does not forget humanity,
and, in his love and mercy,
finds all a mother and a home.

Song

Lord, remember us when you
come into your kingdom.

Blessed are the poor in spirit,
theirs is the kingdom of heaven.
Blessed are those who suffer,
they shall be comforted.
Blessed are the meek,
they shall inherit the earth.

Through the tree Adam was exiled,
but through the tree of the cross
the thief entered Paradise.
Adam disobeyed your will.
The thief crucified with you
confessed in you the hidden God.

Lord, remember us when you
come into your kingdom.

Blessed are those who hunger and thirst for justice,
for in the kingdom to come
they will be satisfied.

From the disciple the transgressors of the Law
bought the creator of the Law,
and led him like a criminal
before Pilate, and they cried out:
"Crucify him! Crucify him!"
because he called himself the Son of God.

Lord, remember us when you
come into your kingdom.

Blessed are the merciful,
for they shall find
mercy.

The crowd loudly cried out:
"Crucify Jesus the Nazarene."
In folly, incited by their leaders,

they sought salvation for Barabbas.
Today we raise our voices on high,
and with the crucified thief we cry out:

Lord, remember us when you
come into your kingdom.

Blessed are the pure in heart,
for they shall see
God.

You were led to the slaughter,
like a lamb before its shearers.
In your heart there was no hatred,
only love and forgiveness for all.
You did not call upon legions of angels,
but you entrusted yourself to the Father.

Lord, remember us when you
come into your kingdom.

Blessed are the people of peace,
they shall be called
children of God.

You were crucified, O Lord,
because you brought true peace
that the world does not know.
Blessed are the feet of those who bring peace,
even if nailed and pierced,
O Christ, Son of the living God.

Lord, remember us when you
come into your kingdom.

Blessed are those persecuted for the cause of justice.
Blessed are you when they insult you,
persecute you and speak lies about you.
Rejoice and exult,
your reward will be great in heaven.

On the cross you bound the tyrant,
the enemy who persecutes humanity,
ransoming us from the chains of death and of evil,
liberating us so that we may live,
O Lord, friend of the people.

Lord, remember us when you
come into your kingdom.

Reading of the Word of God

Alleluia, alleluia, alleluia
(*Lent*: Praise to you, Lord Jesus Christ, king of
    endless glory.)
This is the Gospel of the poor,
liberation for the imprisoned,
sight for the blind,
freedom for the oppressed.

Alleluia, alleluia, alleluia

Alleluia, alleluia, alleluia

The Son of Man came to serve,
whoever wants to be great
should become servant of all.
Alleluia, alleluia, alleluia

Prayers of Intercession

Kyrie eleison, Kyrie eleison, Kyrie eleison

Song to Mary

O do not weep, Mother of God,
beside the Cross of Christ, our Savior.
Be joyful, for truly he is risen;
in his body there lies hidden
all the ransom
and the salvation
of all people. (*3 times*)

Our Father

Prayer for Special Occasions

Prayer with the Apostles

Hymn

Jesus traveled through cities and villages,
preaching the Gospel of the kingdom,
bringing healing to the sick,
while the crowds followed him:

Seeing them like a flock of sheep,
abandoned, and without a shepherd,
he said, "The harvest is great,
but the laborers are few."

Having called to him the Twelve,
he gave them every power
to cast out evil spirits
and heal every kind of sickness.

Their names are Peter and Andrew,
James, John, and Philip,
Bartholomew, Thaddeus, Thomas, and Matthew,
James, Simon, and Judas who then betrayed him.

Blessed is Peter who recognized him:
it was not flesh or blood
that revealed to him that Jesus
was the true Son of God.

Blessed are Peter, James, and John,
on the mountain, together with the Lord,
when his face was transfigured,
and they heard the voice of the Father.

They had left everything
and followed him everywhere.
They will sit with him at the end,
and will receive eternal life.

The leaders dominate the nations,
but among the disciples let it not be like this;
the one who wishes to be great
should become servant of all.

Blessed is Peter who wept
because he was afraid to confess him.
Sad instead is Judas who through fear
sold him for thirty pieces of silver.

Blessed is Paul who, on the road to Damascus,
encountered the Lord.
He had been tenacious for the tradition,
but then announced him to the world.

Of one heart in prayer, the Apostles,
together with the Mother of God,
were filled with the Holy Spirit,
and began to speak to the people.

Psalmody

Reading of the Word of God

Alleluia, alleluia, alleluia
(*Lent*: Praise to you, Lord Jesus Christ, king of
    endless glory.)

If we die with him, we shall live with him,
if with him we endure, with him we shall reign.

Alleluia, alleluia, alleluia

Responsorial Song

We carry this powerful treasure in vessels of clay.
If we are harassed on every side,
we are not crushed.
We carry this powerful treasure in vessels of clay.

If we are overwhelmed,
we do not despair.
We carry this powerful treasure in vessels of clay.

If we are persecuted,
we are not abandoned.
We carry this powerful treasure in vessels of clay.

If we are beaten,
we do not die.
We carry this powerful treasure in vessels of clay.

Because we all live
by the unending power of God.
We carry this powerful treasure in vessels of clay.

Invocations

Kyrie eleison, Kyrie eleison, Kyrie eleison

Our Father

PRAYER OF THE HOLY SPIRIT

Invitatory

> O God, come to our assistance.
> O Lord, make haste to help us.
>
> Glory to the Father, and to the Son, and to
> the Holy Spirit,
> now and forever. Amen. Alleluia.
> (*Lent*: Praise be to you.)

Hymn

> Come thou Holy Spirit
> Send from highest heaven
> Radiance of thy light.
>
> Come, father of the poor
> Come, giver of all gifts
> Come, light of every heart.
>
> Of comforters the best
> Dear guest of every soul
> Refreshment ever sweet.
>
> In our labor rest
> Coolness in our heat
> Comfort in our grief.

O most blessed light
Fill the inmost hearts
Of thy faithful ones.

Without thy holy presence
All is dark
Nothing free from sin.

What is soiled cleanse
What is dry refresh
What is wounded heal.

What is rigid bend
What is frozen warm
Guide what goes astray.

Give thy faithful ones
Who in thee confide
Sevenfold hallowing.

Give goodness its reward
Give journey safe through death
Give joy that has no end.

Reading of the Word of God

Alleluia, alleluia, alleluia
(*Lent*: Praise to you, Lord Jesus Christ, king of
    endless glory.)

If we are not reborn through water and the Spirit,
we cannot enter the kingdom of God.

Alleluia, alleluia, alleluia

Alleluia, alleluia, alleluia
The Spirit of the Lord is upon me,
he sent me to bring good news to the poor.

(*alternatively*)

I will pour out my Spirit on all peoples,
I will raise up prophets among you.

Alleluia, alleluia, alleluia

Song

Sound the trumpet in Zion.
Gather the people together,
assemble the elders and gather the children:
this is the day of the Lord.

O come now all you people,
   come out from your houses,
and gather all together to the Lord;
united heart and soul, we praise his Holy Name,
and the Spirit will renew in us his strength.

Sound the trumpet in Zion . . .

All your older people shall have the gift of dreams
and your younger people shall see visions;
even on the afflicted, and those who are in prison,
shall I pour out my Spirit, in those days.

Sound the trumpet in Zion . . .

O Land, have no more fear: be glad, and rejoice,
because our mighty Lord has done great things;
animals and beasts, do not be afraid
for the pastures of the wilderness are green.

Sound the trumpet in Zion . . .

You children of Zion, be glad in the Lord,
because the autumn rain pours down for you;
who makes the waters flow, and puts an end
    to dryness;
you will eat to your content and have your fill.

Sound the trumpet in Zion . . .

Hammer all your ploughshares, make them
    into swords,
and turn your garden sickles into spears;
all the weak will say, "Now I have found strength!"
and the smallest shall be strong in the Lord.

Sound the trumpet in Zion . . .

Our Father

PRAYER FOR THE SICK

(*Lent*: Prayer of Lent, Hymn of Lent)

Invitatory

O God, come to our assistance.
O Lord, make haste to help us.

Glory to the Father, and to the Son, and to
    the Holy Spirit,
now and forever. Amen. Alleluia.
(*Lent*: Praise be to you.)

Psalm 40

Reading of the Word of God

Alleluia, alleluia, alleluia
(*Lent*: Praise to you, Lord Jesus Christ, king of
    endless glory.)

This is the Gospel of the poor,
liberation for the imprisoned,

sight for the blind,
freedom for the oppressed.

Alleluia, alleluia, alleluia

Introduction to the Memory of Names

To the Lord, good and merciful who can do all
things, we present in prayer the names of our
brothers and sisters and of all those who seek healing
and salvation for their lives.

Kyrie eleison, Kyrie eleison, Kyrie eleison

Concluding Prayer of the Memory of Names

Our Father

Hymn of Hezekiah

O Lord my God
Today I hope in you
Give me life

I said: In the noontide of my days
I must depart
I am consigned to the gates of Sheol
for the rest of my years.

I said: I shall not see the Lord
In the land of the living;
My dwelling is plucked up and removed from me
like a shepherd's tent
You bring me to an end; I cry for help until morning
All my sleep has fled from my soul
My eyes are weary with looking upward.
What can I say? You have done all this.

You have held back my life from the
      pit of destruction
for you have cast all my sins behind your back
For death cannot praise you
The living, the living, they thank you

Today I live and I am here to thank you
Witnessing to all your truth
The Lord saved us: we will sing to
      stringed instruments
All the days of our lives in the house of the Lord.

Embrace of Peace

Final Song

PRAYER OF THE TIME OF CHRISTMAS

Song of the Shepherds

> Shepherds, tell us what you saw:
> Announce who is born on the earth!
>
> You did not see, shepherds, a warrior,
> You did not see legions of men;
> They have chariots and horses,
> He who is born today has the Lord.
>
> Shepherds, tell us what you saw:
> Announce who is born on the earth!
>
> The woman has given birth to a child,
> They have placed him in a manger
> In the city of Bethlehem of Judea
> There was no place for him.
>
> Shepherds, tell us what you saw:
> Announce who is born on the earth!
>
> The child who is born is a sign,
> With him a new heaven arises,
> With him a new earth emerges,
> The time of the Lord has been proclaimed.
>
> Shepherds, tell us what you saw:
> Announce who is born on the earth!

Joseph brought him into the land of Egypt,
But from Egypt the son was called
And he went to live in Nazareth,
And he will be called the Nazarene.

Shepherds, tell us what you saw:
Announce who is born on the earth!

The Spirit of the Lord is upon him,
Who sent him for the poor and blind,
For the prisoners and the contrite of heart:
Today the promise is fulfilled.

Shepherds, tell us what you saw:
Announce who is born on the earth!

Reading of the Word of God

Alleluia, alleluia, alleluia

Glory to God in the highest
and peace on earth to the people he loves.

Alleluia, alleluia, alleluia

Hymn to Christ Savior

Alleluia, alleluia, alleluia

Christ, our savior,
The only son born of the Father;

The Word was made flesh
In the womb of the Virgin Mary;

Alleluia, alleluia, alleluia

You are our eternal hope,
The light and splendor of the Father!
Receive the prayer
of your poor children in this world.

Alleluia, alleluia, alleluia

Today the heavens, earth, and seas
Praise the one who sent you,
Everything that is in them
Exults in seeing your birth.

Alleluia, alleluia, alleluia

On this day we too
Celebrate your coming,
With your blood you redeemed us,
For this we sing a new song.

Alleluia, alleluia, alleluia

Prayers of Intercession

Kyrie eleison, Kyrie eleison, Kyrie eleison

Our Father

Hymn

Adeste Fideles
laeti triumphantes
venite venite
in Bethlehem.
Natum videte
regem angelorum
Venite adoremus, venite adoremus
venite adoremus, Dominum.

PRAYER OF EASTER

Song of Mary at the Tomb

Alleluia, alleluia, alleluia (*2 times*)

Mary was weeping outside the tomb,
I followed Jesus, I truly loved him,
Jesus has healed me and given me life,
and they killed him, he's not here any more.

Alleluia, alleluia, alleluia (*2 times*)

The tomb is empty, the body's not there,
she hears a voice that calls her by name,
and with her face still marked by her tears
she turns around and runs toward him.

Alleluia, alleluia, alleluia (*2 times*)

Why seek the living among the dead?
Stand up and run, I'm not here any more;
you are the least in the eyes of the others;
be first to cry, "He's risen indeed."

Alleluia, alleluia, alleluia (*2 times*)

Hymn of the Resurrection

Alleluia, alleluia, alleluia

Christ is risen from the dead
and will die no more.
Alleluia, alleluia, alleluia

Despite the tomb's heavy stone,
the sorrowful sin of this world,
the guards keeping watch over your body,
you are risen, Lord, our God.

Alleluia, alleluia, alleluia . . .

To the women who came to the tomb,
an angel spoke of your resurrection.
You became the disciples' companion,
and in Emmaus, you broke bread with them.

Alleluia, alleluia, alleluia . . .

Despite the closed doors and fear,
you appeared to the gathered disciples,
gave them power to forgive,
and offered them your peace.

Alleluia, alleluia, alleluia . . .

Today, throughout the world, with faith,
we celebrate your resurrection.
From the depths of our hearts we confess,
you are our Lord and our God.

Alleluia, alleluia, alleluia . . .

Reading of the Word of God

Alleluia, alleluia, alleluia *(solemn)*
Christ is risen from the dead
and will die no more.
He awaits us in Galilee!
Alleluia, alleluia, alleluia

Song of the Light

Come, receive the light
  from the light that does not end.

Your resurrection has enlightened the world.
Come, receive the light
  from the light that does not end.

Darkness and death are put to flight.
Come, receive the light
  from the light that does not end.

Your day has no knowledge of night.
Come, receive the light
  from the light that does not end.

Your light enlightens your servants.
Come, receive the light
  from the light that does not end.

Your love guards your disciples.
Come, receive the light from the light
   that does not end.

(*or*)

Prayers of Intercession

Kyrie eleison, Kyrie eleison, Kyrie eleison

Our Father

Easter Acclamation

Christ is risen!
Very truly he is risen!

Song

Christ is risen! He is risen indeed!
He awaits us in Galilee. (*3 times*)

PRAYER FOR PEACE

Invitatory

O God, come to our assistance.
O Lord, make haste to help us.

Glory to the Father, and to the Son, and to
the Holy Spirit,
now and forever. Amen. Alleluia.
(*Lent*: Praise be to you.)

Psalmody

Reading of the Word of God

Alleluia, alleluia, alleluia
(*Lent*: Praise to you, Lord Jesus Christ, king of
endless glory.)

This is the Gospel of the poor,
liberation for the imprisoned,
sight for the blind,
freedom for the oppressed.

Alleluia, alleluia, alleluia

Alleluia, alleluia, alleluia
The Son of Man came to serve,

whoever wants to be great
should become servant of all.
Alleluia, alleluia, alleluia

Prayer for the Peoples at War

(Reading of the list of countries at war)

Kyrie Eleison

Song of Intercession

O God, come to our assistance.

O Lord, make haste to help us.

Lord, you heard the lament
of your people in Egypt.

Receive the lament
of the oppressed and exiled people.

Make haste to help them
and they will be saved.

Lord, you healed the lepers
who presented themselves before you.

Heal the sick,
be near to those in need.

Make haste to help them
and they will be saved.

You delivered the possessed,
free those who are not masters of themselves.

Make haste to help them
and they will be saved.

You gave sight to the blind
and strength to the paralyzed.

Make everyone able
to see and communicate.

Make haste to help them
and they will be saved.

You called the dead back to life.
You restored them to the light.

Do not allow death to reign,
give back life to your servants.

Make haste to help them
and they will be saved.

You ate with the sinner
and forgave every sin.

Look at our misery and sorrow.
Forgive all our sins.

Come quickly to our help
and we will be saved.

For you are a good God
and a friend of the people.

Our Father

Hymns, Songs, and Prayers of the Community

Song of Introduction

If you have a quarrel with another
before coming to this holy table,
turn back and humbly ask for peace
from the one who has something against you.

If there comes into this holy gathering
someone richly dressed, with rings of gold,
do not give him the better place for this
for the poor are the true friends of God.

If a poor man enters where you gather
who is dressed in rags and has nothing,
do not leave him standing at the back
to give his place to one more important.

If someone believes that he's religious
and speaks, but never stops to listen,
he should realize that this all is vain,
his heart he fills with self-deception.

If you come from the fields or from working,
go and set the table for the Lord,
do not rest until everything is ready;
for we are unworthy to serve him.

Song of Lent

This is the time of return.
Return to me with all your heart,
tear your hearts and not your clothes,
return to me with all your heart.

The son returns to his Father,
"Father I have sinned against you,
I am no longer worthy to be your son."
The son finds a merciful Father.

This is the time of return.
God is merciful and good,

slow to anger and rich in kindness,
he is moved with compassion for you.

The woman weeps on Jesus' feet,
she wipes them with her hair,
her sins are forgiven,
for she has shown great love.

Do not remember the things past,
do not consider things of old.
I do not remember your sins.
Go in peace and sin no more.

Te Deum

We praise thee, O God;
we acknowledge thee to be the Lord.
All the earth doth worship thee,
    the Father everlasting.
To thee all angels cry aloud, the heavens
    and all the powers therein.
To thee cherubim and seraphim continually do cry,

Holy, holy, holy, Lord God of Sabaoth;

Heaven and earth are full of the majesty of thy glory.
The glorious company of the apostles praise thee.
The goodly fellowship of the prophets praise thee.
The noble army of martyrs praise thee.

The holy Church throughout all the world
    doth acknowledge thee:
the Father of an infinite majesty;
thine honorable, true, and only Son;
also the Holy Ghost the Comforter.

Thou art the King of glory, O Christ.
Thou art the everlasting Son of the Father.
When thou tookest upon thee to deliver man,
thou didst not abhor the Virgin's womb.
When thou hadst overcome the sharpness of death,
thou didst open the kingdom of heaven to
    all believers.

Thou sittest at the right hand of God, in the glory
    of the Father.
We believe that thou shalt come to be our judge.
We therefore pray thee, help thy servants,
whom thou hast redeemed with thy precious blood.
Make them to be numbered with thy saints in
    glory everlasting.

O Lord, save thy people and bless thine heritage.
Govern them and lift them up for ever.
Day by day we magnify thee;
and we worship thy name, ever world without end.
Vouchsafe, O Lord, to keep us this day without sin.
O Lord, have mercy upon us, have mercy upon us.

O Lord, let thy mercy lighten upon us, as our
  trust is in thee.
O Lord, in thee have I trusted; let me never
  be confounded.

Hymn of Abraham

Abraham, father of all believers
Who came from Ur of the Chaldeans,
Left from the land of Haran,
And crossed the Euphrates into the desert.

The word of the Lord was addressed to him,
And the promise of a blessing
To become a great people,
A blessing and a curse for many.

Then fear and worry in the night
To find a future heir,
Thus will be his descendants,
They will number as the stars in heaven.

He is the father of Ishmael, the warrior,
And of Isaac, the son of a barren woman,
Three strangers were his guests at Mamre
And he pleaded for the righteous of the city.

Abraham did not hold back his only son
And God always blessed him with life,

He died happy and rich in days
And his children throughout the world bless him.

Final Song

The mountain of the Lord's house
will rise above all other mountains
be raised above the hills
to it shall stream all the nations

Alleluia, alleluia, alleluia

Many peoples shall gather and say
"Come let us go up to the mountain of the Lord
to the house of the God of Jacob
that he may teach us all his ways."

Alleluia, alleluia, alleluia

"We will walk along his paths,
for from Zion will go forth the law,
and the word of the Lord
will be proclaimed from Jerusalem."

Alleluia, alleluia, alleluia

"We will beat our swords into ploughshares
turn our spears into pruning hooks

no longer shall there be division
we will walk in the light of the Lord."

Alleluia, alleluia, alleluia

Prayer of the Community

Lord, our God,
in the confusion
and loneliness of this world,
you do not cease to gather with your word
a holy people
from every land, city, and nation,
so that in charity
they may offer worship pleasing to you.
Keep the flock you have gathered,
preserve it in your love,
now and forever.
Amen.

Prayer for the Sign of Peace

Lord, our God,
make us worthy of your peace
despite our misery.
Let us be joined without fictions,
hypocrisy, or vain interests.
May we be united only by your peace and charity.
Keep our union stable

through the presence of your Spirit,
so that we may witness to the world
the peace which you alone grant,
you who are the God of peace,
of charity,
of forgiveness and mercy,
now and forever.
Amen.

Prayer of the Worthless Servants

Lord, our God,
remember us
your sinful and worthless servants
when we invoke your name.
Sustain us according to your word
and we will have life.
Do not disappoint us in our hope,
but assure the good of your servants.
Make us worthy of loving you
with our whole heart,
that we might always fear you
and in all do your will.
Because you are a good God,
great, and a friend of men and women.
Father, Son, and Holy Spirit,
now and forever,
Amen.

Prayer of Conversion and Forgiveness

Lord Jesus,
who said to the crowds,
"Repent for the kingdom of God is at hand,"
who in your mercy welcomed sinners,
prostitutes, and tax collectors,
who healed people from every kind of illness;
do not look upon our sin,
do not despise the sin of this city,
welcome all of us in your love,
make us pure through your forgiveness,
cleanse us through your Spirit,
show us your face
and we will be saved,
for you are merciful,
full of love for men and women,
now and forever.
Amen.

Prayer of the Light

Lord, our God,
we give thanks to you,
as the day is ending,
for the clarity of this light.
We pray to you
to enlighten our hearts
and to guide our steps

with the light of your Spirit
through the days to come.
Amen.

Prayer of Bidding Farewell

All-powerful Lord,
Father of our Lord Jesus Christ,
bless these your servants,
protect them and sustain them,
make them joyful with your presence.
Guard them and keep them steadfast before you.
Teach them to observe your word,
to walk along your paths,
and to recognize you when they encounter you
poor, weak, and in prison.
Give them a trusting and serene peace,
by the power of your Spirit,
now and forever.
Amen.

Prayer of the Evening

Lord, my God,
my only hope,
do not allow weariness
to impede me from seeking you,
in your presence and among men and women,
but may I always seek

your face with love.
Keep me in your steadfastness,
heal my infirmity,
keep me in your wisdom,
deliver me from my ignorance.
You who opened to me, welcome me,
open the door to me when I knock,
now and forever.
Amen.

Prayer of the Cross

Lord Jesus,
who by your Cross saved the world,
we confess you as friend
and rescuer of people.
Despite our misery and sin,
we will not betray you like Judas,
but like the good thief we pray,
Remember us, O Lord, in your kingdom!
Do not look at our unworthiness:
we were absent, far, forgetful, afraid,
when you were crucified, abandoned,
without consolation.
Teach us, with your eloquent love,
always to follow you along your path,
to carry with you the Cross of your ransom.
You, who are God,

who live and reign,
with the Father almighty,
with the Holy Spirit who is love,
now and forever.
Amen.

Prayer of the Holy Spirit

Father,
send in your name the Holy Spirit
who will teach us everything,
who will remind us of every word of Jesus,
who will stay with us for ever.
The Spirit will console us,
the Spirit will sustain us
along the difficult paths of the world,
the Spirit will lead us to truth
in order to be true in love.
The Spirit will open us to future things,
the Spirit will give us what is
of the Father and of the Son.
Father,
may your Spirit fill the life of each of us,
may your Spirit fill our hearts,
may our community overflow with love,
may prophets arise, may dreams grow,
may mercy spring forth,
may your Spirit flow throughout the world,

may your Spirit blow where he wants,
especially where there is sorrow, loneliness, and cold,
may your Spirit renew the faces of all
    men and women,
renew the hearts of the people,
change the earth.
With faith, with one heart,
Father, we invoke you.
Amen.

Prayer with the Mother of God

Lord, our God,
who, in the womb of the Virgin Mary,
generated the Son of our salvation,
who, every day in the womb of your Church,
ignites the light of life,
do not look at our sins,
but free us from the burden that weighs us down.
Make us ready
to sing, with the Mother of God,
the greatness of your mercy.
Amen.

Prayer of the Trisagion

Accept, O Lord,
this evening prayer
at the end of the day,

in front of the darkness of sin
and the night of this world.
Stay with us,
because evening is coming
and the day is about to end,
you who are light, holy, and joyful,
without end.

Prayer of the Vigil

Lord Jesus,
your word is laid in our hearts,
as you were once laid in the tomb.
You do not find yourself within earth and stone,
but in the lives of your disciples.
You are a God that did not choose to
    entrust yourself
to the legions of angels,
but rather to the faithfulness of your friends.
You are a God who was led to death,
but who has risen to life.
You are a God who went to the Cross
because you love men and women.
Your word is like a seed
which has fallen into our lives.
We pray to you that
the seed bear fruit
and bear it abundantly,

that a great tree will grow,
and welcome the birds of the sky.
Your word has been laid deep within us,
as we remember your passion,
your death on the Cross,
and your resurrection to life.
You will come as Lord,
in the light of your day,
Christ, dead and risen.
We pray,
do not delay, Lord,
accept the prayer of your servants
who wait for you
like Martha and Mary,
who invoke you
like the widow from Nain,
because you are the Lord of life.
At the end of these days,
on the threshold of your day,
do not look on our guilt,
release us from our sins,
and bring us into your kingdom of peace and justice,
now and forever. Amen.

Litany of Sunday

Lord,
in your love

guard your disciples,
preserve your family,
illumine our footsteps.

Kyrie eleison, Kyrie eleison, Kyrie eleison

Lord, forgive
all who today confessed their sin,
asked for pardon,
and sought mercy.

Kyrie eleison, Kyrie eleison, Kyrie eleison

Lord, speak with strength
to those who have not listened to you,
move through the hearts of men and women,
so that you may be known.

Kyrie eleison, Kyrie eleison, Kyrie eleison

Lord, come as shepherd,
where hatred and division are,
where darkness, death, and violence reign.

Kyrie eleison, Kyrie eleison, Kyrie eleison

Lord, in your holy liturgy,
we have confessed you risen.
Remain with us and with those
who have celebrated you in faith.
Preserve us in your light,

because this day is about to end.
Remain with us,
even though it is evening,
because you have risen.
O friend of the people,
now and forever,
Amen.

Prayer of the Multiplication of Bread

Lord Jesus,
you listened to your disciples,
at the end of their day,
you spoke to the crowds of the kingdom of God,
you healed those needing care;
at the closing of the day,
in a deserted place,
you ordered the disciples to feed the people.
Where will we find the bread?
Where will we find the strength?
Blessed is the Lord,
who multiplies the bread,
who is present among his own.
Accept the offering of your disciples,
the pains and expectations of these days,
and, for us, multiply your love.
Amen.

Prayer of the Cross for the Deceased

We pray to the crucified Lord

>for the life of every person.

Kyrie eleison, Kyrie eleison, Kyrie eleison

We pray to the Lord of life, who died on the Cross. We pray for those who die, for the poor man Lazarus, that after so much suffering he may have his reward; and for the rich man, who feasted lavishly, that he may return to his senses.

Kyrie eleison, Kyrie eleison, Kyrie eleison

We pray to the Lord for every person, so that each may live in love and, like Simeon, may go in peace, after having seen the light that comes to illuminate the nations.

Kyrie eleison, Kyrie eleison, Kyrie eleison

We pray to the Lord, so that death may have no more power over those

who have been ransomed by his resurrection.

Kyrie eleison, Kyrie eleison, Kyrie eleison

We pray to the Lord, so that all people will no longer have their life cut off by the violence of others, by exploitation, by hatred.

Kyrie eleison, Kyrie eleison, Kyrie eleison

We pray to the Lord, so that all may love, respect, and defend life, while expecting and preparing for the kingdom of God.

Kyrie eleison, Kyrie eleison, Kyrie eleison

We pray to the Lord, who through the resurrection of Lazarus consoled Martha and Mary, so that by his resurrection he may console those who have seen death strike so brutally around them.

Kyrie eleison, Kyrie eleison, Kyrie eleison

We pray to the Lord, who left one hundred sheep to search for the lost one, to care for our brother/sister. For we can do no more for him/her, but to entrust him/her to the Lord's mercy.

Kyrie eleison, Kyrie eleison, Kyrie eleison

O Lord,

you wept at the tomb of your friend Lazarus,
you were moved before the sorrow of humankind;
accompany with your love
the one who has left us;
say only a word
and death will be conquered.
You are a God of the living,
Spirit of life, now and forever.
Amen.

Prayer of the Cross

> Lord Jesus,
> who died powerless,
> bound to the Cross,
> without saving yourself,
> you who have saved so many,
> turn your eyes upon us,
> have pity on us,
> forgive us
> from occasions of avarice, of pride, of arrogance;
> free us from the temptation
> to save our own life;
> help us to lose our life
> for your sake and the Gospel;
> you who are risen
> and sit at the right hand of the Father,
> now and forever.
> Amen.

Prayer of Benediction

> Blessed are you, Lord, our rock.
> You have upheld the foundation of our life.
> You have saved our soul
> from loneliness and pride,
> from sin and evil.
> You have made for us a good life,
> participants in your house,

on the path of your will.
Bless the days of our past
with your forgiveness.
Bless our future
unto eternity.
Bless our community,
and render us fruitful in your love,
now and in the days to come.
Amen.

Prayer of Advent

Lord,
rock of our community,
sustain us in your love,
renew us with your Spirit,
open our hearts to welcome you,
help us to make our community beautiful
so that it may welcome you and our brothers
    and sisters,
make us capable of communicating you to everyone.
Lord,
thank you for having welcomed us into your
    covenant,
making us your family,
brothers and sisters,
your friends,

witnesses of your Advent,
of your coming amongst us.
Amen.

Papal Address on the Fortieth Anniversary of Sant'Egidio

The following address was given by Pope Benedict XVI on April 7, 2008, in the Basilica of Saint Bartholomew on the Tiber Island, in honor of the Sant'Egidio community's fortieth anniversary:

Dear brothers and sisters,

We can consider this meeting of ours in the ancient basilica of St. Bartholomew on the Tiber Island as a pilgrimage in memory of the martyrs of the twentieth century, innumerable men and women, known and unknown, who shed their blood for the Lord throughout the century. Our pilgrimage is guided by the Word of God. Like a lamp to our steps, like a light on our way (cf. Ps 119:105), it illuminates the life of every believer. My beloved Predecessor, John Paul II, specifically destined this temple to be a place of memory for the martyrs of the twentieth century, and he entrusted it to the Community of Sant'Egidio, which this year gives thanks to the Lord for the fortieth anniversary of its beginning. I warmly greet the Cardinals and Bishops who take part in this Liturgy. I greet Professor Andrea Riccardi, the founder of the Community of Sant'Egidio, and I thank him for his words; I greet Professor Marco Impagliazzo, the President of the Community; the Assistant, Mgr Matteo Zuppi; and Mgr Vincenzo Paglia, Bishop of Terni, Narni and Amelia.

In this place, so full of memories, we ask ourselves: why did these brother martyrs of ours not seek to save at all costs the irreplaceable gift of life? Why did they continue to serve the Church, in spite of severe threats and intimidations? In this basilica, where the relics of the Apostle Bartholomew are kept, where the remains of St. Adalbert are worshipped, we hear the echo of the eloquent witness of those people who lived with love, not only in the twentieth century but since the very beginning of the Church, offering in martyrdom their lives to Christ. In the icon on the high altar that portrays some of these witnesses of faith, the words of the Revelation stand out: "These are they who have come out of the great tribulation" (Rev 7:13). The elder asking who the ones in white robes are and where they come from is told that "they have washed their robes and made them white in the blood of the Lamb" (Rev 7:14). It sounds like a strange answer. But in the coded language of the Seer of Patmos it contains a precise reference to the white flame of love which urged Christ to shed his blood for us. By virtue of that blood we were purified. Supported by that flame, the martyrs, too, shed their blood and were purified by love: by the love of Christ that made them capable of sacrificing themselves for love. Jesus said: "No one has greater love than this: to lay down his life for his friends" (Jn 15:13). All the witnesses of faith live this "greater" love, and following the example of the divine Master, they are ready to sacrifice their lives for the Kingdom. Thus one becomes a friend of Christ, conformable to Him, by accepting the extreme sacrifice, setting no borders to the gift of love and the service of faith.

Stopping at the six altars that remember the Christians who fell under the totalitarian violence of Communism and Nazism, the ones killed in America, in Asia and Oceania, in Spain and Mexico, and in Africa, we ideally halt in front of the many sorrowful events of the past century. Many Christians fell while they carried out the evangelizing mission of the Church: their blood was mixed with that of the native Christians whom faith was communicated to. Others, often in situations where Christians were a minority, were killed out of hatred of the faith. Finally, many immolated themselves, fearless of threats and perils, in order not to abandon the needy, the poor, and the believers that were entrusted to their care. They are Bishops, priests, religious men and women, lay believers. They are many! The Servant of God John Paul II, during the jubilee ecumenical celebration for the new martyrs held on 7th May 2000 at the Coliseum, said that these brothers and sisters in faith of ours are like a magnificent fresco of the Christian humanity in the twentieth century, a fresco of the Beatitudes lived to the point of shedding one's blood. And he used to repeat that the witness of Christ, even to the point of shedding his blood, speaks with a voice more powerful than the divisions of the past.

It is true: violence, totalitarianism, persecution, blind brutality seemingly appear the strongest, silencing the voice of the witnesses of faith. From a human perspective, they appear to be the defeated of history. But the risen Jesus illuminates their witness, and thus we understand the meaning of martyrdom. Tertullian says in this regard: "*Plures efficimur quoties metimur a vobis: sanguis martyrum semen christianorum* – We multiply even while you reap us: the blood of the martyrs is the seed of new Christians" (Apol. 50,13: CCL 1,171). In their defeat, in the humiliation of people who suffer for the Gospel, there is a power the world knows not: "When I am weak, then I am strong" – says the Apostle Paul (2 Cor 12:10). It is the power of love, defenseless and victorious even in seeming defeat. This power challenges and defeats death.

Even this twenty-first century opened under the sign of martyrdom. When Christians are really the leaven, the light and salt of the earth, like Jesus, they also become the object of persecution; like Him, they are a "sign of contradiction." The brotherly coexistence, love, faith, and preferential option for the little ones and the poor that characterize the existence of Christian communities sometimes arouse violent hostility. How useful it is, then, to look at the luminous witness of the ones who came before us under the sign of heroic faithfulness to the point of martyrdom! And in this ancient basilica, thanks to the care of the Community of Sant'Egidio, the memory of many witnesses of faith, who have fallen in recent times, is kept and worshipped. Dear friends of the Community of Sant'Egidio, turning your eyes to these heroes of faith, strive to imitate their courage and perseverance in serving the Gospel, especially among the poor. Be builders of peace and reconciliation among enemies and people who oppose each other. Nourish your faith by meditating and listening to the Word of God, through daily prayer, by actively taking part in the Holy Mass. Authentic friendship with Christ will be the source of your mutual love. Supported by his Spirit, you will contribute to building a more brotherly world. May the Holy Virgin, the Queen of the Martyrs, support you and help you to be authentic witnesses of Christ. Amen!

For Further

Information

U p-to-date news and information about the Community of Sant'Egidio and its programs can be found at **www.santegidio.org/en**. This website also contains daily commentaries that offer a compliment to this book and invite readers to join the community along its path.

If you are interested in knowing more or becoming part of the community in the United States, please contact:

Community of St. Egidio USA, P.O. Box 250 299, New York, NY 10026; tel/fax (212) 663-1483; e-mail: **santegidiousa@gmail.com**

Notes

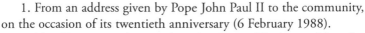

1. From an address given by Pope John Paul II to the community, on the occasion of its twentieth anniversary (6 February 1988).

2. The Christian is always a disciple of Jesus. This state of discipleship does not change with the passing of the years, with responsibilities, with the knowledge of the scriptures and of the life of the church. The correct attitude of the Christian is always that of a disciple. In the closing passages of the Gospel of John (Jn 21:15–23) there is a dialogue between Jesus and Simon: After having received from the Lord the task of tending his flock, Simon asks Jesus about the future of the disciple Jesus loved, John, and Jesus says to him: "If it is my will that he remain until I come, what is that to you? Follow me!" By saying *follow me,* he confirms that Simon Peter always remains first of all a disciple who must follow the master.

3. The stories of Simon Peter are not simply stories meant to commemorate the leader of the early community, he who first exercised a ministry. They are stories in which every Christian can discover his or her own personal story. For example, in the sixth chapter of the Gospel of John, after Jesus calls himself "the bread of life," many disciples begin to leave him. As they are leaving, Jesus turns to the twelve and asks them: "Do you also wish to go away?" Simon Peter answers him, "Lord, to whom can we go? You have the words of eternal life. We have come to believe and know that you are the Holy One of God" (Jn 6:66–70). Simon Peter is shown here as an ordinary disciple of the Lord: weak, but also faithful to the Master. Or take the tradition of the martyrdom of Peter in Rome, during the persecution. This

story shows that this "weak" disciple had indeed gone a long way from Galilee, a province, to preach the Gospel in the great capital of the Roman Empire, so different and unsettling compared to his small homeland. The Lord had earlier said to him: "Very truly, I tell you, when you were younger, you used to fasten your own belt and to go wherever you wished. But when you grow old, you will stretch out your hands, and someone else will fasten a belt around you and take you where you do not wish to go." The evangelist adds, "He said this to indicate the kind of death by which he would glorify God" (Jn 21:18–19). To live as a mature Christian, Simon would first have to stretch out his hands toward the Lord through an attitude of prayer and listening before Jesus. Eventually, he would have to go everywhere the Gospel was calling him—a long, long way from the little life in Capernaum and of fishing on the lake. Peter became, first of all, a disciple who follows his master, and then a disciple who confirms the other disciples. We are called, as Peter was, to follow Jesus a long way.

4. Forgiveness is crucial in Christian life. The heart of the preaching of Jesus is the call to request forgiveness for our own sins. The true disciple of Jesus is like the tax collector in Luke's Gospel (Lk 18:9–14), a man who in Jesus' time would have been considered a sinner and would have been despised both for his scandalous behavior and from an economic point of view. But the tax collector is very different from the Pharisee, who feels righteous. Regarding this, we read the following in the parable of the Pharisee and the tax collector in the Gospel of Luke: "For all who exalt themselves will be humbled, but all who humble themselves will be exalted" (Lk 18:14). True life in the community is characterized by forgiveness, so much so that the community must help its brothers and sisters to correct themselves, as is written in the words of Jesus in the Gospel of Matthew (Mt 18:15–35). The life of each individual Christian in the world is characterized by forgiveness as well. The Christian is like that "wicked servant" of whom so much has been forgiven and who must in turn

forgive those whom he meets (Mt 18:21–35). The sinners who ask forgiveness for their sins have the sure grace of receiving forgiveness both in the confession of their sins and in the sacrament of reconciliation: "Truly I tell you, whatever you bind on earth will be bound in heaven, and whatever you loose on earth will be loosed in heaven" (Mt 18:18).

5. "The Church has always venerated the divine Scriptures just as she venerates the body of the Lord, since, especially in the sacred liturgy, she unceasingly receives and offers to the faithful the bread of life from the table both of God's word and of Christ's body" (*Dei Verbum* VI, 21). The Church venerates the word of God in the scriptures that are the heart of its prayer, as can be seen in the Eucharistic liturgy, where the community listens to the reading of the Gospel and of texts from the New and Old Testament.

6. Sometimes, our sin, the life we have led until meeting with the Lord, our character, our origin, our culture, are often considered an obstacle to becoming disciples of the Lord, despite our desire. In the pages of the scripture there are many examples of disciples who were far from the Lord. Everything seemed to point to them being considered unfit to follow him, but eventually they follow him. The clearest case is that of the apostle Paul, who played such a major part in the Christian preaching during the church's early years. Paul was a persecutor of the Christians: he even guarded the robes of the murderers during the stoning of a disciple, Stephen, an act which he strongly approved of (Acts 7:58–8:1). The story of his conversion shows that nothing can separate us from the love of God.

7. Patience is a decisive factor in Christian life. In the teachings of Jesus to his disciples, he insists on patience, even in consideration of the difficulties that Christians will have to face throughout their lives. Jesus does not depict Christian life as the absence of labor and suffering. Disciples will suffer for their witness to the Gospel and for the different life they decide to lead. The life of Gospel faithfulness is not a medicine that takes away pain and difficulty. It is not a product

that provides "well-being." Suffering and difficulty braid the life of all, whatever their life choices end up being—it is enough to look at illness, something everyone must deal with, to see that this is so. Jesus says, however, that difficulties and suffering do not prevail, nor will they enslave the men and women who believe in him. The image of the "suffering Christ" expresses the strength of the patience of the Son of God, who believes that the Father will never abandon him. Violence, anger, and aggression are born in impatient hearts that wish to win and are afraid to lose. Jesus is the model of patience, not only in his passion, but also with his disciples, with the crowds, and with those who were looking for him. In the Letter to the Hebrews we read, "Consider him who endured such hostility against himself from sinners, so that you may not grow weary or lose heart" (Heb 12:3).

8. From the beatitudes of the Gospel of Matthew (Mt 5), meekness is central in the life of the Christian. Jesus is gentle and humble in heart. It is the impression that people had of him, even in the moment of his entry into Jerusalem amidst the celebrations of the crowd. The evangelist who portrays this image quotes the prophet Zechariah: "Lo, your king comes to you; triumphant and victorious is he, humble and riding on a donkey" (Zec 9:9). Jesus says: "Blessed are the meek, for they will inherit the earth" (Mt 5:5). It is an expression taken from Psalm 37:11. Meekness and kindness, not violence or arrogance, are the ways in which the disciples will inherit the earth.

9. The word "conversion" is a translation of the words *conversio* (Latin) and *metanoia* (Greek). *Conversio* means literally to "to change direction," like in the case of the two disciples who were going to Emmaus but then returned to Jerusalem. *Metanoia* means to go *beyond* one's habitual way of thinking. That is, to give our mind, our personality, and current way of life a real review and to allow ourselves to be transformed in our thinking and living. As the Gospels were written in Greek, the word *metanoia* was the original word for what has come to be known as conversion.

10. Self-love (which Maximus the Confessor calls *filautia* in Greek) often carries us away from real joy and from what is truly good in our lives. Jesus teaches us not to let self-love rule our lives with expressions that may shock us out of mediocrity, such as the one in the Gospel of Luke: "Whoever comes to me and does not hate father and mother, wife and children, brother and sister, yes, even life itself, cannot be my disciple" (Lk 14:26). Why such a strong word as "hate"? Jesus wants to express discipleship with him as the opposite of self-love—it is a new and totally different kind of love.

11. The disciple is, first of all, the one who listens to the word of the Lord. But the disciple is also one who does it. At the end of the Sermon on the Mount, Jesus calls his people to be real disciples, that is, ones who hear his words and act on them. Such people are compared to a man who has built his house on the rock so that nothing would be able to tear it down (Mt 7:21–27). The "rock" is both hearing and doing. Those who hear but do not act are like the foolish man who has built his house on the sand. In addition, the Letter of James (Jas 1:22) insists on the need of not deceiving ourselves by living as forgetful listeners of the word of the Lord.

12. In the Gospel of Mark we find this same episode of the relatives of Jesus but with details that are slightly different from those of Luke (Mk 3:31–35). Many who approach the four Gospels for the first time are astonished by the differences between them and want to know why these differences exist. We must not be surprised that the four Gospels report similar episodes in different ways—they are like four great windows from which we see the life of Jesus through differing angles and perspectives. The stories are much the same, but are presented in different ways. How did this occur? At the beginning there was the oral preaching, or the "Kerygma," which means the core of the proclamation of the Gospel. The Kerygma represents the memory of the words of the Master and the events of his life. Peter's speech to the people of Jerusalem, after Pentecost, is a typical example of this form of preaching. Subsequently, when the witnesses of the life of Jesus began

to die, the communities put into writing the words and the deeds of the Master. Thus began the development of compilations written by the "evangelists," who are listed as community members in St. Paul's letters, together with apostles, pastors, teachers, and prophets (Eph 4:11–13). The first three Gospels, since the second century, have been attributed to the evangelists Matthew, Mark, and Luke, writers who probably used earlier sources and compilations to craft their work. The first three Gospels are called "Synoptic" because of their similarity. There are, however, real differences between the three. Mark feels very immediate and straight-forward. Matthew is much more organized. Luke, in which emerges the sensitive soul of the author, contains many of the best-loved parables, such as the Prodigal Son and the Good Samaritan. The fourth Gospel, John, is a much more complex work than the previous three Gospels. In it, we sense the personal vision of the author, the "disciple that Jesus loved." The fourth Gospel is a meditation that calls the disciple to believe in the truth that is Jesus. The four Gospels present four different views from which to see Jesus: they complement one another and, most of all, they help us to listen to Jesus with faith and by means of the witness of those who have met him and believed in him.

13. Baptism is the first of the sacraments, and it is the one that is common to all Christians. In baptism, we receive the Holy Spirit, we are freed from original sin, and we become part of the church. In the earliest communities, the church of the first century, baptism was usually received by adults, as is mentioned in the Acts of the Apostles (Acts 8:12–13, 36–39; 10:44–48; 16:14–15), although there is talk in scripture of whole families being baptized, which could have included children and infants (Acts 16:15, 33). It is only from the fifth/sixth centuries, however, that the baptism of infants became common custom.

14. Since the year 2000, the year of the Great Jubilee, the Community of Sant'Egidio has dedicated the Church of St. Bartholomew on the Tiber Island to the memory of the martyrs and witnesses of faith

of the twentieth century. To them is dedicated the great icon above the central altar, while in the lateral chapels are kept the relics of the martyrs and witnesses of faith victims of violence against believers in specific historical moments and areas of the world.

15. Regarding this, one can see the instructions that the apostle Paul gives to the community in Corinth for the celebration of the supper of the Lord (1 Cor 11:17–34), in which the apostle repeats that in the Eucharist, the community eats the body of the Lord and drinks his blood. These instructions of the apostle show that the celebration of the Eucharist is a sacrament that the church always celebrated with great veneration, considering it the highest moment of its prayer and the most authentic moment in which the community gathers together with the Lord.

16. Insistent and faithful prayer, done both as community and individually, means much to the Lord. Hence, both the community gathered together and the individual brothers and sisters must call on the Lord faithfully and ask that his Spirit be given to their own community and to every community so as to deliver them from evil. In these prayers, they must always remember those who are in need: the poor, the suffering, countries at war. They must pray for peace in every part of the world. They are called to pray for the church as well: their own diocese, their bishop, for all the churches, and especially for the Pope.

17. Love is, according to the apostle Paul, a gift that the Holy Spirit pours into the hearts of the family: "God's love has been poured into our hearts through the Holy Spirit that has been given to us" (Rom 5:5). Love is therefore the way in which disciples can imitate the Father: "Be merciful, just as your Father is merciful" (Lk 6:36). One can also look at the words of the apostle in the "hymn to love" in the First Letter to the Corinthians (1 Cor 13), which offers a powerful statement as to how love is to be lived out.

18. Jesus performs miracles in all of the Gospels. He raises the dead, he heals the lepers, the deaf, the lame, the sick, the possessed.

These suffering people are still here today along our streets. Of course, we realize today that many of those the Gospel calls "possessed" are people who suffer from mental illness, people with obsessions, and those suffering interiorly. We have today a new awareness of these things as diseases. But that does not make them go away: the reality is that people continue to suffer from them. And today, as then, disciples are called to overcome their limitations in faith and love to help men and women to be freed from their pain. Miracles are not simply events recounted in the Gospels.

19. Acting on the Gospel of Luke (14:12–14), since 1982 the Community of Sant'Egidio has organized a Christmas banquet for the poor, welcoming homeless and poor people in the Basilica of Santa Maria in Trastevere. Through the years all the communities of Sant'Egidio in the world have celebrated Christmas with the poor as a sign of their belonging to the community's family.

20. St. Paul, in the Letter to the Corinthians, reminds the community: "Consider your own call, brothers and sisters: not many of you were wise by human standards, not many were powerful, not many were of noble birth. But God chose what is foolish in the world to shame the wise; God chose what is weak in the world to shame the strong; God chose what is low and despised in the world, things that are not, to reduce to nothing things that are, so that no one might boast in the presence of God" (1 Cor 1:26–29).

21. The indwelling of God is a theme present throughout the Bible. In front of the temple built by human hands, the believer asks himself how God can live in it. The Gospel of John, in the so-called Prologue (chapter 1), shows how God came to dwell in the person of Jesus: "And the word became flesh and lived among us" (Jn 1:14). The faithful community will experience that the Lord lives in its midst. The risen Christ appears to his disciples and stays with them. In the letter to the church of Laodicea, the Book of Revelation says, "Listen! I am standing at the door, knocking; if you hear my voice and open the door, I will come in to you and eat with you, and you with me"

(Rev 3:20). When the community listens to the word of God, he comes in its midst and has supper with it. The community of the poor disciples in the world becomes the dwelling of God.

References

Berthold, George C., ed. *Maximus Confessor: Selected Writings: Classics of Western Spirituality*. Mahwah, NJ: Paulist Press, 1985.

Bonhoeffer, Dietrich. *Psalms, The Prayer Book of the Bible*. Minneapolis, MN: Augsburg Fortress, 1974.

Holmes, Michael W., ed. *The Apostolic Fathers in English*, 3rd ed. Ada, MI: Baker Academic, 2006.

Solov'ev, Vladimir. "I fondamenti spirituali della vita," presentazione di Olivier Clément, traduzione dal russo di Maria Campatelli e Mar'iana Prokopovy, Roma, Lipa, 1998.

The Community of Sant'Egidio was founded in Rome in 1968 by a group of high school students led by Andrea Riccardi. A lay association of the Catholic Church, Sant'Egidio is today made up of over sixty thousand members living in more than seventy countries worldwide. Its main activities are prayer, service to the poor, ecumenism, and interfaith dialogue. The community is especially known for its work with the elderly, AIDS patients, and the homeless. In recent years, Sant'Egidio has gained the international spotlight for its role as peacemaker in war-torn regions of the world.